SPORTS
AFIELD

SURVIVE!

150 Tips, Tactics, & True Tales

Willow Creek
P R E S S

BIBLIOGRAPHICAL NOTES

From the Little Colorado to the Foot of the Grand Canyon. Excerpted from *The Exploration of the Colorado River and its Canyons*, by John Wesley Powell. First published 1895. Adventure Classics. Washington, DC: National Geographic.

Fremont's Disastrous Fourth Expedition. By Micajah McGehee. *Outdoor Life* magazine 1910.

The Journey Down the Kooskooskee. Excerpted from *In the Heart of the Bitterroot Mountains: The Story of the Carlin Hunting Party of 1893*, by Heclawa (Abraham Himmelwright). New York: G.P. Putnam's Sons. 1895.

Northern Lives. *Outdoor Life*, August 1923.

Captured by the Indians. Excerpted from *Three Years Among the Camanches*, by Nelson Lee. Albany: Baker Taylor. 1859.

Title page illustration: detail from painting, An Unexpected Guest by Philip R. Goodwin. Courtesy of the Coeur d'Alene Art Auction. All other art © ArtClip.com

Published by Willow Creek Press
P.O. Box 147, Minocqua, Wisconsin 54548
www.willowcreekpress.com

Printed in the United States of America

Stories

All acorns (oak nuts) are edible, though many contain bitter tannic acid that should first be removed by boiling or leeching in water. (May 01, p.34)

To relieve the pain of bee stings, which are acidic, apply a paste of baking soda and water; for wasp and hornet stings, which are alkaline, apply or soak in vinegar, lemon, or cranberry juice. (June 01, p.16)

For up to an hour or more after its death, a rattlesnake, operating on sheer nervous reflex, can bite and inject venom. (May 01, p.94)

Lightning travels at a speed of 50,000 miles per second, and hits ground somewhere on earth about 100 times each second. (August 00, p.26)

"It felt like somebody dropped a boulder on my head. [There was a] crackling sound right in the center of my skull."
—Ray Risho, lightning survivor

The odds of accidental gun death are 3,074 to one, and the odds of that shot being hunting related are about as high as those of being struck by lightning. Hunting remains one of the safest of all sports. (Winter 00-01, p.28)

One study estimated that about a third of all tree-stand hunters will fall from a stand some time; of that third, about three percent will suffer crippling injuries. (November 00, p.92)

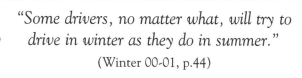

"Some drivers, no matter what, will try to drive in winter as they do in summer." (Winter 00-01, p.44)

On slick surfaces, turning the steering wheel as you brake can result in skidding or possibly even losing control of your vehicle. (Winter 00-01, p.14)

Are you a *survivor*? If you embody these traits, you're more apt to survive a deadly situation. History shows that survivors are primarily those who can: 1. Stay calm and focused. 2. Make both quick and reasoned decisions on a course of action and response. 3. Adapt and improvise. 4. Endure hardships. 5. Recognize dangers and fears while remaining optimistic. 6. Retain, even against all apparent odds, a mindset that refuses to give up—an inner voice that says 'I will survive.' (Summer 97, p.100)

Improvisation and grit: When his station wagon plunged 150 feet off an embankment in Washington State in September 1977, John Vihtelic spent 16 days trapped in a creekbottom, pinned inside the wreckage. Without food or the ability to move anything but his arms, Vihtelic screamed unsuccessfully for help, puncturing a lung in the process. Realizing that rescue might be a long way off, he tore out dashboard wiring and wove it into a rope, which he attached to cloth ripped from the ceiling. With this device he could cast the fabric into nearby Riley Creek, then pull it back and suck out the moisture. This bit of improvising kept him alive long enough to chisel himself free with a rock and a tire iron, though not in time to save his crushed left foot, which had to be amputated. But prosthesis did not stop him from running the frigid Antarctica Marathon this year. (Summer 97, p.103)

Although hypothermia—the dangerous loss of internal body heat—most often occurs gradually over a period of hours, in severe weather an under-protected person can literally freeze to death in as little as 20 to 30 minutes. (February 01, p.16)

Using an Analog Watch. With a wristwatch that has an hour hand and is running on correct time, simply point the hour hand directly toward the sun. South will be halfway between the hour hand and 12. (July 95, p.71)

According to one survey, forty percent of lost hunters mistakenly follow drainages, thinking that they will help them find their way to safety. (October 00, p.42)

From the Little Colorado to the Foot of the Grand Canyon

by John Wesley Powell

Powell's expedition down the Green and Colorado Rivers in 1869 was one of the greatest feats of exploration in American history, covering 1,000 miles of water over 98 days. The one-armed Civil War veteran led his brother and eight other men through the unexplored canyon country in several leaky wooden boats with only rudimentary equipment. As the party finally entered the Grand Canyon, it had already faced a series of harrowing adventures. What had begun months before as a surveying expedition quickly became a fight for survival as starvation loomed and the rapids grew in size between sheer canyon walls.

AUGUST 13.—WE ARE NOW READY TO START on our way down the Great unknown. Our boats, tied to a common stake, chafe each other as they are tossed by the fretful river. They ride high and buoyant, for their loads are lighter than we could desire. We have but a month's rations remaining. The flour has been resifted through the mosquito-net sieve; the spoiled bacon has been dried and the worst of it

7

boiled; the few pounds of dried apples have been spread in the sun and reshrunken to their normal bulk. The sugar has all melted and gone on its way down the river. But we have a large sack of coffee. The lightening of the boats has this advantage: they will ride the waves better and we shall have but little to carry when we make a portage.

We are three quarters of a mile in the depths of the earth, and the great river shrinks into insignificance as it dashes its angry waves against the walls and cliffs that rise to the world above; the waves are but puny ripples, and we but pygmies, running up and down the sands or lost among the boulders.

We have an unknown distance yet to run, an unknown river to explore. What falls there are, we know not; what rocks beset the channel, we know not; what walls rise over the river, we know not. Ah, well! we may conjecture many things. The men talk as cheerfully as ever; jests are bandied about freely this morning; but to me the cheer is somber and the jests are ghastly.

With some eagerness and some anxiety and some misgiving we enter the canyon below and are carried along by the swift water through walls which rise from its very edge. They have the same structure that we noticed yesterday—tiers of irregular shelves below, and, above these, steep slopes to the foot of marble cliffs. We run six miles in a little more than half an hour and emerge into a more open portion of the canyon, where high hills and ledges of rock intervene between the river and the distant walls. Just at the head of this open place the river runs across a dike; that is, a fissure in the rocks, open to depths below, was filled with eruptive matter, and this on cooling was harder than the rocks through which the crevice was made, and when these were washed away the harder volcanic matter remained as a wall, and the river has cut a gateway through it several hundred feet high and as many wide. As it crosses the wall, there is a fall below and a bad rapid, filled with boulders of trap; so we stop to make a portage. Then on we go, gliding by hills and ledges, with distant walls in view; sweeping past sharp angles of rock; stopping at a few points to examine rapids, which we find can be run, until we have made another five miles, when we land for dinner.

Then we let down with lines over a long rapid and start again. Once more the walls close in, and we find ourselves in a narrow gorge, the water again filling the channel and being very swift. With great care and constant watchfulness we proceed, making about four miles this afternoon, and camp in a cave.

August 14.—At daybreak we walk down the bank of the river, on a little sandy beach, to take a view of a new feature in the canyon. Heretofore hard rocks have given us bad river; soft rocks, smooth water; and a series of rocks harder than any we have experienced sets in. The river enters the gneiss! We can see but a little way into the granite gorge, but it looks threatening.

After breakfast we enter on the waves. At the very introduction it inspires awe. The canyon is narrower than we have ever before seen it; the water is swifter; there are but few broken rocks in the channel; but the walls are set, on either side, with pinnacles and crags; and sharp, angular buttresses, bristling with wind- and wave-polished spires, extend far out into the river.

Ledges of rock jut into the stream, their tops sometimes just below the surface, sometimes rising a few or many feet above; and island ledges and island pinnacles and island towers break the swift course of the stream into chutes and eddies and whirlpools. We soon reach a place where a creek comes in from the left, and, just below, the channel is choked with boulders, which have washed down this lateral canyon and formed a dam, over which there is a fall of 30 or 40 feet; but on the boulders foothold can be had, and we make a portage. Three more such dams are found. Over one we make a portage; at the other two are chutes through which we can run.

As we proceed the granite rises higher, until nearly a thousand feet of the lower part of the walls are composed of this rock.

9

About eleven o'clock we hear a great roar ahead, and approach it very cautiously. The sound grows louder and louder as we run, and at last we find ourselves above a long, broken fall, with ledges and pinnacles of rock obstructing the river. There is a descent of perhaps 75 or 80 feet in a third of a mile, and the rushing waters break into great waves on the rocks, and lash themselves into a mad, white foam. We can land just above, but there is no foothold on either side by which we can make a portage. It is nearly a thousand feet to the top of the granite; so it will be impossible to carry our boats around, though we can climb to the summit up a side gulch and, passing along a mile or two, descend to the river. This we find on examination; but such a portage would be impracticable for us, and we must run the rapid or abandon the river. There is no hesitation. We step into our boats, push off, and away we go, first on smooth but swift water, then we strike a glassy wave and ride to its top, down again into the trough, up again on a higher wave, and down and up on waves higher and still higher until we strike one just as it curls back, and a breaker rolls over our little boat. Still on we speed, shooting past projecting rocks, till the little boat is caught in a whirlpool and spun round several times. At last we pull out again into the stream. And now the other boats have passed us. The open compartment of the "Emma Dean" is filled with water and every breaker rolls over us. Hurled back from a rock, now on this side, now on that, we are carried into an eddy, in which we struggle for a few minutes, and are then out again, the breakers still rolling over us. Our boat is unmanageable, but she cannot sink, and we drift down another hundred yards through breakers—how, we scarcely know. We find the other boats have turned into an eddy at the foot of the fall and are waiting to catch us as we come, for the men have seen that our boat is swamped. They push out as we come near and pull us in against the wall. Our boat bailed, on we go again.

The walls now are more than a mile in height—a vertical distance difficult to appreciate. Stand on the south steps of the Treasury building in Washington and look down Pennsylvania

Avenue to the Capitol; measure this distance overhead, and imagine cliffs to extend to that altitude, and you will understand what is meant; or stand at Canal Street in New York and look up Broadway to Grace Church, and you have about the distance; or stand at Lake Street bridge in Chicago and look down to the Central Depot, and you have it again.

A thousand feet of this is up through granite crags; then steep slopes and perpendicular cliffs rise one above another to the summit. The gorge is black and narrow below, red and gray and flaring above, with crags and angular projections on the walls, which, cut in many places by side canyons, seem to be a vast wilderness of rocks. Down in these grand, gloomy depths we glide, ever listening, for the mad waters keep up their roar; ever watching, ever peering ahead, for the narrow canyon is winding and the river is closed in so that we can see but a few hundred yards, and what there may be below we know not; so we listen for falls and watch for rocks, stopping now and then in the bay of a recess to admire the gigantic scenery; and ever as we go there is some new pinnacle, some crag or peak, some distant view of the upper plateau, some strangely shaped rock, or some deep, narrow side canyon.

Then we come to another broken fall, which appears more difficult than the one we ran this morning. A small creek comes in on the right, and the first fall of the water is over boulders, which have been carried down by this lateral stream. We land at its mouth and stop for an hour or two to examine the fall. It seems possible to let down with lines, at least a part of the way, from point to point, along the righthand wall. So we make a portage over the first rocks and find footing on some boulders below. Then we let down one of the boats to the end of her line, when she reaches a corner of the projecting rock, to which one of the men clings and steadies her while I examine an eddy below. I think we can pass the other boats down by us and catch them in the eddy. This is soon done, and the men in the boats in the eddy pull us to their side. On the shore of this little eddy there is about two feet of gravel beach above the water. Standing on this beach, some of the men take the line of the little boat and let it drift down against another projecting angle. Here is a little shelf, on which a man from my boat climbs, and a shorter line is passed to him, and he fastens the boat to the side of the cliff; then the second one is let down, bringing the line of the third. When the second boat is tied up, the two men standing on the beach above spring into the last boat, which is pulled up alongside of ours; then we let down the boats for 25 or 30 yards by walking along the shelf, landing them again in the mouth of a side canyon. Just below this there is another pile of boulders, over which we make another portage. From the foot of these rocks we can climb to another shelf, 40 or 50 feet above the water.

On this bench we camp for the night. It is raining hard, and we have no shelter, but find a few sticks which have lodged in the rocks, and kindle a fire and have supper. We sit on the rocks all night, wrapped in our *ponchos*, getting what sleep we can.

August 15.—This morning we find we can let down for 300 or 400 yards, and it is managed in this way: we pass along the wall by climbing from projecting point to point, sometimes near the water's edge, at other places 50 or 60 feet above, and hold the boat with a line while two men remain aboard and prevent her from being dashed against the rocks and keep the line from getting caught on the wall. In two hours we have brought them all down, as far as it is possible, in this way. A few yards below, the river strikes with great violence against a projecting rock and our boats are pulled up in a little bay above. We must now manage to pull out of this and clear the point below. The little boat is held by the bow obliquely up the stream. We jump in and pull out only a few strokes, and sweep clear of the dangerous rock. The other boats follow in the same manner and the rapid is passed.

It is not easy to describe the labor of such navigation. We must prevent the waves from dashing the boats against the cliffs. Sometimes, where the river is swift, we must put a bight of rope about a rock, to prevent the boat from being snatched from us by a wave; but where the plunge is too great or the chute too swift, we just let her leap and catch her below or the undertow will drag her under the falling water and sink her. Where we wish to run her out a little way from shore through a channel between rocks, we first throw in little sticks of driftwood and watch their course, to see where we must steer so that she will pass the channel in safety. And so we hold, and let go, and pull, and lift, and ward—among rocks, around rocks, and over rocks.

And now we go on through this solemn, mysterious way. The river is very deep, the canyon very narrow, and still obstructed, so that there is no steady flow of the stream; but the waters reel and roll and boil, and we are scarcely able to determine where we can go. Now the boat is carried to the right, perhaps close to the wall; again, she is shot into the stream, and perhaps is dragged over to the other side, where, caught in a whirlpool, she spins about. We can neither land nor run as we please. The boats are entirely unmanageable; no order in their running can be preserved; now one, now another, is ahead, each crew laboring for its own preservation. In such a place we come to another rapid. Two of the boats run it perforce. One succeeds in landing, but there is no foothold by which to make a portage and she is pushed out again into the stream. The next minute a great reflex wave fills the open compartment; she is water-logged, and drifts unmanageable. Breaker after breaker rolls over her and one capsizes her. The men are thrown out; but they cling to the boat, and she rifts down some distance alongside of us and we are able to catch her. She is soon bailed out and the men are aboard once more; but the oars are lost, and so a pair from the "Emma Dean" is spared.

Then for two miles we find smooth water. Clouds are playing in the canyon today. Sometimes they roll down in great masses, filling the gorge with gloom; sometimes they hang aloft from wall to wall and cover the canyon with a roof of impending storm, and we can peer long distances up and down this canyon corridor, with its cloud-roof overhead, its walls of black granite, and its river bright with the sheen of broken waters. Then a gust of wind sweeps down a side gulch and, making a rift in the clouds, reveals the blue heavens, and a stream of sunlight pours in. Then the clouds drift away into the distance, and hang around crags and peaks and pinnacles and towers and walls, and cover them with a mantle that lifts from time to time and sets them all in sharp relief. Then baby clouds creep out of side canyons, glide around points, and creep back again into more distant gorges. Then clouds arrange in strata across the canyon, with intervening vista views to cliffs and rocks beyond. The clouds are children of the heavens, and when they play among the rocks they lift them to the region above.

It Rains! Rapidly little rills are formed above, and these soon grow into brooks, and the brooks grow into creeks and tumble over the walls in innumerable cascades, adding their wild music to the roar of the river. When the rain ceases the rills, brooks, and creeks run dry. The waters that fall during a rain on these steep rocks are gathered at once into the river; they could scarcely be poured in more suddenly if some vast spout ran from the clouds to the stream itself. When a storm bursts over the canyon a side gulch is dangerous, for a sudden flood may come, and the inpouring waters will raise the river so as to hide the rocks.

Early in the afternoon we discover a stream entering from the north—a clear, beautiful creek, coming down through a gorgeous red canyon. We land and camp on a sand beach above its mouth, under a great, overspreading tree with willow-shaped leaves.

August 16.—We must dry our rations again today and make oars.

The Colorado is never a clear stream, but for the past three or four days it has been raining much of the time, and the floods poured over the walls have brought down great quantities of mud, making it exceedingly turbid now. The little affluent which we have discovered here is a clear, beautiful creek, or river, as it would be termed in this western country, where streams are not abundant. We have named one stream, away above, in honor of the great chief of the "Bad Angels," and as this is in beautiful contrast to that, we conclude to name it "Bright Angel."

Early in the morning the whole party starts up to explore the

Bright Angel River, with the special purpose of seeking timber from which to make oars. A couple of miles above we find a large pine log, which has been floated down from the plateau, probably from an altitude of more than 6,000 feet, but not many miles back. On its way it must have passed over many cataracts and falls, for it bears scars in evidence of the rough usage which it has received. The men roll it on skids, and the work of sawing oars is commenced.

This stream heads away back under a line of abrupt cliffs that terminates the plateau, and tumbles down more than 4,000 feet in the first mile or two of its course; then runs through a deep, narrow canyon until it reaches the river.

Late in the afternoon I return and go up a little gulch just above this creek, about 200 yards from camp, and discover the ruins of two or three old houses, which were originally of stone laid in mortar. Only the foundations are left, but irregular blocks, of which the houses were constructed, lie scattered about. In one room I find an old mealing-stone, deeply worn, as if it had been much used. A great deal of pottery is strewn around, and old trails, which in some places are deeply worn into the rocks, are seen.

It is ever a source of wonder to us why these ancient people sought such inaccessible places for their home. They were, doubtless, an agricultural race, but there are no lands here of any considerable extent that they could have cultivated. To the west of Oraibi, one of the towns in the Province of Tusayan, in northern Arizona, the inhabitants have actually built little terraces along the face of the cliff where a spring gushes out, and thus made their sites for gardens. It is possible that the ancient inhabitants of this place made their agricultural lands in the same way. But why should they seek such spots? Surely the country was not so crowded with people as to demand the utilization of so barren a region. The only solution suggested of the problem is this: We know that for a century or two after the settlement of Mexico many expeditions were sent into the country now comprising Arizona and New Mexico, for the purpose of bringing the town-building people under the dominion of the Spanish fled to regions at that time unknown; and there are traditions among the people who inhabit the pueblos that still remain that the canyons were these unknown lands. It may be these buildings were erected at that time; sure it is that they have a much more modern appearance than the ruins scattered over Nevada, Utah, Colorado, Arizona, and New Mexico. Those old Spanish conquerors had a monstrous greed for gold and a wonderful lust for saving souls. Treasures they must have, if not on earth, why, then, in heaven; and when they failed to find heathen temples bedecked with silver, they propitiated Heaven by seizing the heathen themselves. There is yet extant a copy of a record made by a heathen artist to express his conception of the demands of the conquerors. In one part of the picture we have a lake, and near by stands a priest pouring water on the head of a native. On the other side, a poor Indian has a cord about his throat. Lines run from these two groups to a central figure, a man with beard and full Spanish panoply. The interpretation of the picture-writing is this: "Be baptized as this saved heathen, or be hanged as that damned heathen." Doubtless, some of these people preferred another alternative, and rather than be baptized or hanged they chose to imprison themselves within these canyon walls.

August 17. — Our rations are still spoiling; the bacon is so badly injured that we are compelled to throw it away. By an accident, this morning, the saleratus was lost overboard. We have now only musty flour sufficient for ten days and a few dried apples, but plenty of coffee. We must make all haste possible. If we meet with difficulties such as we have encountered in the canyon above, we may be compelled to give up the expedition and try to reach the Mormon settlements to the north. Our hopes are that the worst places are passed, but our barometers are all so much injured as to be useless, and so we have lost our reckoning in altitude, and know not how much descent the river has yet to make.

The stream is still wild and rapid and rolls through a narrow channel. We make but slow progress, often landing against a wall and climbing around some point to see the river below. Although very anxious to advance, we are determined to run with great caution, lest by another accident we lose our remaining supplies. How precious that little flour has become! We divide it among the boats and carefully store it away, so that it can be lost only by the loss of the boat itself.

We make ten miles and a half, and camp among the rocks on the right. We have had rain from time to time all day, and have been thoroughly drenched and chilled; but between showers the sun shines with great power and the mercury in our thermometers stands at 115°, so that we have rapid changes from great extremes, which are very disagreeable. It is especially cold in the rain tonight. The little canvas we have is rotten and useless; the rubber ponchos with which we started from Green River City have all been lost; more than half the party are without hats, not one of us has an entire suit of clothes, and we have not a blanket apiece. So we gather driftwood and build a fire; but after supper the rain, coming down in torrents, extinguishes it, and we sit up all night on the rocks, shivering, and are more exhausted by the night's discomfort than by the day's toil.

August 18.—The day is employed in making portages and we advance but two miles on our journey. Still it rains.

While the men are at work making portages I climb the granite to its summit and go away back over the rust-colored sandstones and greenish-yellow shales to the foot of the marble wall. I climb so high that the men and boats are lost in the black depths below and the dashing river is a rippling brook, and still there is more canyon above than below. All about me are interesting geologic records. The book is open and I can read as I run. All about me are grand views, too, for the clouds are playing again in the gorges. But somehow I think of the nine days' rations and the bad river, and the lesson of the rocks and the glory of the scene are but half conceived.

I push on to an angle, where I hope to get a view of the country beyond, to see if possible what the prospect may be of our soon running through this plateau, or at least of meeting with some geologic change that will let us out of the granite; but, arriving at the point, I can see below only a labyrinth of black gorges.

August 19.—Rain again this morning. We are in our granite prison still, and the time until noon is occupied in making a long, bad portage.

After dinner, in running a rapid the pioneer boat is upset by a wave. We are some distance in advance of the larger boats. The river is rough and swift and we are unable to land, but cling to the boat and are carried down stream over another rapid. The men in the boards above see our trouble, but they are caught in whirlpools and are spinning about in eddies, and it seems a long time before they come to our relief. At last they do come; our boat is turned right side up and bailed out; the oars, which fortunately have floated along in company with us, are gathered up, and on we go, without even landing. The clouds break away and we have sunshine again.

Soon we find a little beach with just room enough to land. Here we camp, but there is no wood. Across the river and a little way above, we see some driftwood lodged in the rocks. So we bring two boat loads over, build a huge fire, and spread everything to dry. It is the first cheerful night we have had for a week—a warm, drying fire in the midst of the camp, and a few bright stars in our patch of heavens overhead.

August 20.—The characteristics of the canyon change this morning. The river is broader, the walls more sloping, and composed of black slates that stand on edge. These nearly vertical slates are washed out in places—that is, the softer beds are washed out between the harder, which are left standing. In this way curious little alcoves are formed, in which are quiet bays of water, but on a much smaller scale than the great bays and buttresses of Marble Canyon.

The river is still rapid and we stop to let down with lines several times, but make greater progress, as we run ten miles. We camp on the right bank. Here, on a terrace of trap, we discover another group of ruins. There was evidently quite a village on this rock. Again we find mealing-stones and much broken pottery, and up on a little natural shelf in the rock back of the ruins we find a globular basket that would hold perhaps a third of a bushel. It is badly broken, and as I attempt to take it up it falls to pieces. There are many beautiful flint chips, also, as if this had been the home of an old arrow-maker.

August 21.—We start early this morning, cheered by the prospect of a fine day and encouraged also by the good run made yesterday. A quarter of a mile below camp the river turns abruptly to the left, and between camp and that point is very swift, running down in a long, broken chute and piling up against the foot of the cliff, where it turns to the left. We try to pull across, so as to go down on the other side, but the waters are swift and it seems impossible for us to escape the rock below; but, in pulling across, the bow of the boat is turned to the farther shore, so that we are swept broadside down and are prevented by the rebounding waters from striking against the wall. We toss about for a few seconds in these billows and are then carried past the danger. Below, the river turns again to the right, the canyon is very narrow, and we see in advance but a short distance. The water, too, is very swift, and there is no landing-place. From around this curve there comes a mad roar, and down we are carried with a dizzying velocity to the head of another rapid. On either side high over our heads there are overhanging granite walls, and the sharp bends cut off our view, so that a few minutes will carry us into unknown waters. Away we go on one long, winding chute. I stand on deck, supporting myself with a strap fastened on either side of the gunwale. The boat glides rapidly where the water is smooth, then, striking a wave, she leaps and bounds like a thing of life, and we have a wild, exhilarating ride for ten miles, which we make in less than an hour. The excitement is so great that we forget the danger until we hear the roar of a great fall below; then we back on our oars and are carried slowly toward its head and succeed in landing just above and find that we have to make another portage. At this we are engaged until some time after dinner.

19

Just here we run out of the granite. Ten miles in less than half a day, and limestone walls below. Good cheer returns; we forget the storms and the gloom and the cloud-covered canyons and the black granite and the raging river, and push our boats from shore in great glee.

Though we are out of the granite, the river is still swift, and we wheel about a point again to the right, and turn, so as to head back in the direction from which we came; this brings the granite in sight again, with its narrow gorge and black crags; but we meet with no more great falls or rapids. Still, we run cautiously and stop from time to time to examine some places which look bad. Yet we make ten miles this afternoon; twenty miles in all today.

August 22.—We come to rapids again this morning and are occupied several hours in passing them, letting the boats down from rock to rock with lines for nearly half a mile, and then have to make a long portage. While the men are engaged in this I climb the wall on the northeast to a height of about 2,500 feet, where I can obtain a good view of a long stretch of canyon below. Its course is to the southwest. The walls seem to rise very abruptly for 2,500 or 3,000 feet, and then there is a gently sloping terrace on each side for two or three miles, when we again find cliffs, 1,500 or 2,000 feet high. From the brink of these the plateau stretches back to the north and south for a long distance. Away down the canyon on the right wall I can see a group of mountains, some of which appear to stand on the brink of the canyon. The effect of the terrace is to give the appearance of a narrow winding valley with high walls on either side and a deep, dark, meandering gorge down its middle. It is impossible from this point of view to determine whether or not we have granite at the bottom; but from geologic considerations, I conclude that we shall have marble walls below.

After my return to the boats we run another mile and camp for the night. We have made but little over seven miles today, and a part of our flour has been soaked in the river again.

August 23.—Our way today is again through marble walls. Now and then we pass for a short distance through patches of granite, like hills thrust up into the limestone. At one of these places we have to make another portage, and, taking advantage of the delay, I go up a little stream to the north, wading it all the way, sometimes having to plunge in to my neck, in other places being compelled to swim across little basins that have been excavated at the foot of the falls. Along its course are many cascades and springs, gushing out from the rocks on either side. Sometimes a cottonwood tree grows over the water. I come to one beautiful fall, of more than 150 feet, and climb around it to the right on the broken rocks. Still going up, the canyon is found to narrow very much, being but 15 or 20 feet wide; yet the walls rise on either side many hundreds of feet, perhaps thousands; I can hardly tell.

In some places the stream has not excavated its channel down vertically through the rocks, but has cut obliquely, so that one wall overhangs the other. In other places it is cut vertically above and obliquely below, or obliquely above and vertically below, so that it is impossible to see out overhead. But I can go no farther; the time which I estimated it would take to make the portage has almost expired, and I start back on a round trot, wading in the creek where I must and plunging through basins. The men are waiting for me, and away we go on the river.

Just after dinner we pass a stream on the right, which leaps into the Colorado by a direct fall of more than 100 feet, forming a beautiful cascade. There is a bed of very hard rock above, 30 or 40 feet in thickness, and there are much softer beds below. The hard beds above project many yards beyond the softer, which are washed out, forming a deep cave behind the fall, and the stream pours through a narrow crevice above into a deep pool below. Around on the rocks in the cavelike chamber are set beautiful ferns, with delicate fronds and enameled stalks. The frondlets have their points turned down to form spore cases. It has very much the appearance of the maidenhair fern, but is much larger. This delicate foliage covers the rocks all about the fountain, and gives the chamber great beauty. But we have little time to spend in admiration; so on we go.

We make fine progress this afternoon, carried along by a swift river, shooting over the rapids and finding no serious obstructions. The canyon walls for 2,500 or 3,000 feet are very regular, rising almost perpendicularly, but here and there set with narrow steps, and occasionally we can see away above the broad terrace to distant cliffs.

We camp tonight in a marble cave, and find on looking at our reckoning that we have run 22 miles.

August 24.—The canyon is wider today. The walls rise to a vertical height of nearly 3,000 feet. In many places the river runs under a cliff in great curves, forming amphitheaters half-dome shaped.

Though the river is rapid, we meet with no serious obstructions and run 20 miles. How anxious we are to make up our reckoning every time we stop, now that our diet is confined to plenty of coffee, a very little spoiled flour, and very few dried apples! It has come to be a race for a dinner. Still, we make such fine progress that all hands are in good cheer, but not a moment of daylight is lost.

August 25. — We make 12 miles this morning, when we come to monuments of lava standing in the river—low rocks mostly, but some of them shafts more than a hundred feet high. Going on down three or four miles, we find them increasing in number. Great quantities of cooled lava and many cinder cones are seen on either side; and then we come to an abrupt cataract. Just over the fall on the right wall a cinder cone, or extinct volcano, with a well-defined crater, stands on the very brink of the canyon. This, doubtless, is the one we saw two or three days ago. From this volcano vast floods of lava have been poured down into the river, and a stream of molten rock has run up the canyon three or four miles and down we know not how far. Just where it poured over the canyon wall is the fall. The whole north side as far as we can see is lined with the black basalt, and high up on the opposite wall are patches of the same material, resting on the benches and filling old alcoves and caves, giving the wall a spotted appearance.

The rocks are broken in two along a line which here crosses the river, and the beds we have seen while coming down the canyon for the last 30 miles have dropped 800 feet on the lower side of the line, forming what geologists call a "fault." The volcanic cone stands directly over the fissure thus formed. On the left side of the river, opposite, mammoth springs burst out of this crevice, 100 or 200 feet above the river, pouring in a stream quite equal in volume to the Colorado Chiquito.

This stream seems to be loaded with carbonate of lime, and the water, evaporating, leaves an incrustation on the rocks; and this process has been continued for a long time, for extensive deposits are noticed in which are basins with bubbling springs. The water is salty.

We have to make a portage here, which is completed in about three hours; then on we go.

We have no difficulty as we float along, and I am able to observe the wonderful phenomena connected with this flood of lava. The canyon was doubtless filled to a height of 1,200 or 1,500 feet, perhaps by more than one flood. This would dam the water back; and in cutting through this great lava bed, a new channel has been formed, sometimes on one side, sometimes on the other. The cooled lava, being of firmer texture that the rocks of which the walls are composed, remains in some places; in others a narrow channel has been cut, leaving a line of basalt on either side. It is possible that the lava cooled faster on the sides against the walls and that the center ran out; but of this we can only conjecture. There are other places where almost the whole of the lava is gone, only patches of it being seen where it has caught on the walls. As we float down we can see that it ran out into side canyons. In some places this basalt has a fine, columnar structure, often in concentric prisms, and masses of these concentric columns have coalesced. In some places, when the flow occurred the canyon was probably about the same depth that it is now, for we can see where the basalt has rolled out on the sands, and—what seems curious to me—the sands are not melted or metamorphosed to any appreciable extent. In places

23

the bed of the river is of sandstone or limestone, in other places of lava, showing that it has all been cut out again where the sandstones and limestones appear; but there is a little yet left where the bed is of lava.

What a conflict of water and fire there must have been here! Just imagine a river of molten rock running down into a river of melted snow. What a seething and boiling of the waters; what clouds of steam rolled into the heavens!

Thirty-five miles today. Hurrah!

August 26.—The canyon walls are steadily becoming higher as we advance. They are still bold and nearly vertical up to the terrace. We still see evidence of the eruption discovered yesterday, but the thickness of the basalt is decreasing as we go down stream; yet it has been reinforced at points by streams that have come down from volcanoes standing on the terrace above, but which we cannot see from the river below.

Since we left the Colorado Chiquito we have seen no evidences that the tribe of Indians inhabiting the plateaus on either side ever come down to the river; but about eleven o'clock today we discover an Indian garden at the foot of the wall on the right, just where a little stream with a narrow flood plain comes down through a side canyon. Along the valley the Indians have planted corn, using for irrigation the water which bursts out in springs at the foot of the cliff. The corn is looking quite well, but it is not sufficiently advanced to give us roasting ears; but there are some nice green squashes. We carry ten or a dozen of these on board our boats and hurriedly leave, not willing to be caught in the robbery, yet excusing ourselves by pleading our great want. We run down a short distance to where we feel certain no Indian can follow, and what a kettle of squash sauce we make! True, we have no salt with which to season it, but it makes a fine addition to our unleavened bread and coffee. Never was fruit so sweet as these stolen squashes.

After dinner we push on again and make fine time, finding many rapids, but none so bad that we cannot run them with safety; and when we stop, just at dusk, and foot up our reckoning, we find we have run 35 miles again. A few days like this, and we are out of prison.

We have a royal supper—unleavened bread, green squash sauce, and strong coffee. We have been for a few days on half rations, but now have no stint of roast squash.

August 27.—This morning the river takes a more southerly direction. The dip of the rocks is to the north and we are running rapidly into lower formations. Unless our course changes we shall very soon run again into the granite. This gives some anxiety. Now and then the river turns to the west and excites hopes that are soon destroyed by another turn to the south. About nine o'clock we come to the dreaded rock. It is with no little misgiving that we see the river enter these black, hard walls. At its very entrance we have to make a portage; then let down with lines past some ugly rocks. We run a mile or two farther, and then the rapids below can be seen.

About eleven o'clock we come to a place in the river which seems much worse than any we have yet met in all its course. A little creek comes down from the left. We land first on the right and clamber up over the granite pinnacles for a mile or two, but can see no way by which to let down, and to run it would be sure destruction. After dinner we cross to examine on the left. High above the river we can walk along on the top of the granite, which is broken off at the edge and set with crags and pinnacles, so that it is very difficult to get a view of the river at all. In my eagerness to reach a point where I can see the roaring fall below, I go too far on the wall, and can neither advance nor retreat. I stand with one foot on a little projecting rock and cling with my hand fixed in a little crevice. Finding I am caught here, suspended 400 feet above the river, into which I must fall if my footing fails, I call for help. The men come and pass me a line, but I cannot let go of the rock long enough to take hold of it. Then they bring two

25

or three of the largest oars. All this takes time which seems very precious to me; but as last they arrive. The blade of one of the oars is pushed into a little crevice in the rock beyond me in such a manner that they can hold me pressed against the wall. Then another is fixed in such a way that I can step on it; and thus I am extricated.

Still another hour is spent in examining the river from this side, but no good view of it is obtained; so now we return to the side that was first examined, and the afternoon is spent in clambering among the crags and pinnacles and carefully scanning the river again. We find that the lateral streams have washed boulders into the river, so as to form a dam, over which the water makes a broken fall of 18 or so feet; then there is a rapid, beset with rocks, for 200 or 300 yards, while on the other side, points of the wall project into the river. Below, there is a second fall; how great, we cannot tell. Then there is a rapid, filled with huge rocks, for 100 or 200 yards. At the bottom of it, from the right wall, a great rock projects quite halfway across the river. It has a sloping surface extending up stream, and the water, coming down with all the momentum gained in the falls and rapids above, rolls up this inclined plane many feet, and tumbles over to the left. I decide that it is possible to let down over the first fall, then run near the right cliff to a point just above the second, where we can pull out into a little chute, and, having run over that in safety, if we pull with all our power across the stream, we may avoid the great rock below. On my return to the boat I announce to the men that we are to run it in the morning. Then we cross the river and go into camp for the night on some rocks in the mouth of the little side canyon.

After supper Captain Howland asks to have a talk with me. We walk up the little creek a short distance, and I soon find that his object is to remonstrate against my determination to proceed. He thinks that we had better abandon the river here. Talking with him, I learn that he, his brother, and William Dunn have determined to go no farther in the boats. So we return to camp. Nothing is said to the other men.

As soon as I determine all this, I spread my plot on the sand and wake Howland, who is sleeping down by the river, and show him where I suppose we are, and where several Mormon settlements are situated.

We have another short talk about the morrow, and he lies down again; but for me there is no sleep. All night long I pace up and down a little path, on a few yards of sand beach, along by the river; Is it wise to go on? I go to the boats again to look at our rations. I feel satisfied that we can get over the danger immediately before us; what there may be below I know not. From our outlook yesterday on the cliffs, the canyon seemed to make another great bend to the south, and this, from our experience heretofore, means more and higher granite walls. I am not sure that we can climb out of the canyon here, and, if at the top of the wall, I know enough of the country to be certain that it is a desert of rock and sand between this and the nearest Mormon town, which, on the most direct line, must be 75 miles away. True, the late rains have been favorable to us, should we go out, for the probabilities are that we shall find water still standing in holes; and at one time I almost conclude to leave the river. But for years I have been contemplating this trip. To leave the exploration unfinished, to say that there is a part of the canyon which I cannot explore, having already nearly accomplished it, is more than I am willing to acknowledge, and I determine to go on.

I wake my brother and tell him of Howland's determination, and he promises to stay with me; then I call up Hawkins, the cook, and he makes a like promise; then Sumner and Bradley and Hall, and they all agree to go on.

August 28. — At last daylight comes and we have breakfast without a word being said about the future. The meal is as solemn as a funeral. After breakfast I ask the three men if they still think it best to leave us. The elder Howland thinks it is, and Dunn agrees with him. The younger Howland tries to persuade them to go on with the party; failing in which, he decides to go with his brother.

Then we cross the river. The small boat is very much disabled and unseaworthy. With the loss of hands, consequent on the departure of the three men, we shall not be able to run all of the boats; so I decide to leave my Emma Dean.

Two rifles and a shotgun are given to the men who are going out. I ask them to help themselves to the rations and take what they think to be a fair share. This they refuse to do, saying they have no fear but that they can get something to eat; but Billy, the cook, has a pan of biscuits prepared for dinner, and these he leaves on a rock.

Before starting, we take from the boat our barometers, fossils, the minerals, and some ammunition and leave them on the rocks. We are going over this place as light as possible. The three men help us lift our boats over a rock 25 or 30 feet high and let them down again over the first fall, and now we are all ready to start. The last thing before leaving, I write a letter to my wife and give it to Howland. Sumner gives him his watch, directing that it be sent to his sister should he not be heard from again. The records of the expedition have been kept in duplicate. One set of these is given to Howland; and now we are ready. For the last time they entreat us not to go on, and tell us that it is madness to set out in this place; that we can never get safely through it; and, further, that the river turns again to the south into the granite, and a few miles of such rapids and falls will exhaust our entire stock of rations, and then it will be too late to climb out. Some tears are shed; it is rather a solemn parting; each party thinks the other is taking the dangerous course.

My old boat left, I go on board of the "Maid of the Canyon." The three men climb a crag that overhangs the river to watch us off. The "Maid of the Canyon" pushes out. We glide rapidly along the foot of the wall, just grazing one great rock, then pull out a little into the chute of the second fall and plunge over it. The open compartment is filled when we strike the first wave below, but we cut through it, and then the men pull with all their power toward the left wall and swing clear of the dangerous rock below all right. We are scarcely a minute in running it, and find that, although it looked bad from above, we have passed many places that were worse.

The other boat follows without more difficulty. We land at the first practicable point below, and fire our guns, as a signal to the men above that we have come over in safety. Here we remain a couple of hours, hoping that they will take the smaller boat and follow us. We are behind a curve in the canyon and cannot see up to where we left them, and so we wait until their coming seems hopeless, and then push on.

And now we have a succession of rapids and falls until noon, all of which we run in safety. Just after dinner we come to another bad place. A little stream comes in from the left, and below there is a fall, and still below another fall. Above, the river tumbles down, over and among the rocks, in whirlpools and great waves, and the waters are lashed into mad, white foam. We run along the left, above this, and soon see that we cannot get down on this side, but it seems possible to let down on the other. We pull up stream again for 200 or 300 yards and cross. Now there is a bed of basalt on this northern side of the canyon, with a bold escarpment that seems to be a hundred feet high. We can climb it and walk along its summit to a point where we are just at the head of the fall. Here the basalt is broken down again, so it seems to us, and I direct the men to take a line to the top of the cliff and let the boats down along the wall. One man remains in the boat to keep her clear of the rocks and prevent her line from being caught on the projecting angles. I climb the cliff and pass along to a point just over the fall and descend by broken rocks, and find that the break of the fall is above the break of the wall, so that we cannot land, and that still below the river is very bad, and that there is no possibility of a portage. Without waiting further to examine and determine what shall be done, I hasten back to the top of the cliff to stop the boats from coming down. When I arrive I find the men have let one of them down to the head of the fall. She is in swift water and they are not able to pull her back; nor are they able to go on with the line, as it is not long enough to reach the higher part of the cliff which is just before them; so they take a bight around a crag. I send two men back for the other line. The boat is in very swift water, and Bradley is standing in the open compartment, holding out his oar to prevent her from striking against the foot of the cliff. Now she shoots out into the stream and up as far as the line will permit, and then, wheeling, drives headlong against the rock, and then out and back again, now straining on the line, now striking against the rock. As soon as the second line is brought, we pass it down to him; but his attention is all taken up with his own situation, and he does not see that we are passing him the line. I stand on a projecting rock, waving my hat to gain his attention, for my voice is drowned by the roaring of the falls. Just at this moment I see him take his knife from its sheath and step forward to cut the line. He has evidently decided that it is

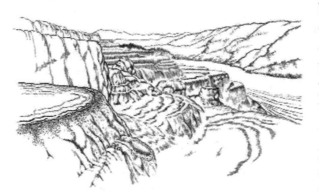

better to go over with the boat as it is than to wait for her to be broken to pieces. As he leans over, the boat sheers again into the stream, the stempost breaks away and she is loose. With perfect composure Bradley seizes the great scull oar, places it in the stern rowlock, and pulls with all his power (and he is an athlete) to turn the bow of the boat down stream, for he wishes to go bow down, rather than to drift broadside on. One, two strokes he makes, and a third just as she goes over, and the boat is fairly turned, and she goes down almost beyond our sight, though we are more than a hundred feet above the river. Then she comes up again on a great wave, and down and up, then around behind some great rocks, and is lost in the mad, white foam below. We stand frozen with fear, for we see no boat. Bradley is gone! so it seems. But now, away below, we see something coming out of the waves. It is evidently a boat. A moment more, and we see

Bradley standing on deck, swinging his hat to show that he is all right. But he is in a whirlpool. We have the stem-post of his boat attached to the line. How badly she may be disabled we know not. I direct Sumner and Powell to pass along the cliff and see if they can reach him from below. Hawkins, Hall, and myself run to the other boat, jump aboard, push out, and away we go over the falls. A wave rolls over us and our boat is unmanageable. Another great wave strikes us, and the boat rolls over, and tumbles and tosses, I know not how. All I know is that Bradley is picking us up. We soon have all right again, and row to the cliff and wait until Sumner and Powell can come. After a difficult climb they reach us. We run two or three miles farther and turn again to the northwest, continuing until night, when we have run out of the granite once more.

August 29.—We start very early this morning. The river still continues swift, but we have no serious difficulty, and at twelve o'clock emerge from the Grand Canyon of the Colorado. We are in a valley now, and low mountains are seen in the distance, coming to the river below. We recognize this as the Grand Wash.

A few years ago a party of Mormons set out from St. George, Utah, taking with them a boat, and came down to the Grand Wash, where they divided, a portion of the party crossing the river to explore the San Francisco Mountains. Three men— Hamblin, Miller, and Crosby—taking the boat, went on down the river to Callville, landing a few miles below the mouth of the Rio Virgen. We have their manuscript journal with us, and so the stream is comparatively well known.

Tonight we camp on the left bank, in a mesquite thicket.

The relief from danger and the joy of success are great. When he who has been chained by wounds to a hospital cot until his canvas tent seems like a dungeon cell, until the groans of those who lie about tortured with probe and knife are piled up, a weight of horror on his ears that he cannot throw off, cannot forget, and until the stench of festering wounds and anesthetic drugs has filled the air with its loathsome burden,—when he at last goes out into the open field, what a world he sees! How beautiful the sky, how bright the sunshine, what "floods of delirious music" pour from the throats of birds, how sweet the fragrance of earth and tree and blossom! The first hour of convalescent freedom seems rich recompense for all pain and gloom and terror.

Something like these are the feelings we experience tonight. Ever before us has been an unknown danger, heavier than immediate peril. Every waking hour passed in the Grand Canyon has been one of toil. We have watched with deep solicitude the steady disappearance of our scant supply of rations, and from time to time have seen the river snatch a portion of the little left, while we were a-hungered. And danger and toil were endured in those gloomy depths, where ofttimes clouds hid the sky by day and but a narrow zone of stars could be seen at night. Only during the few hours of deep sleep, consequent on hard labor, has the roar of the waters been hushed. Now the danger is over, now the toil has ceased, now the gloom has disappeared, now the firmament is bounded only by the horizon, and what a vast expanse of constellations can be seen!

The river rolls by us in silent majesty; the quiet of the camp is sweet; our joy is almost ecstasy. We sit till long after midnight talking of the Grand Canyon, talking of home, but talking chiefly of the three men who left us. Are they wandering in those depths, unable to find a way out? Are they searching over the desert lands above for water? Or are they nearing the settlements?

[The three men who left the party were killed by Indians.]

Pocket lint—an emergency fire starting kit necessity? Yes. Collect a resealable sandwich bag full of this flame starter, light with a metal match, and find yourself relaxed by an open fire in almost any conditions. (June 01, p. 12)

In addition to lifesaving warmth, emergency fires can be used to purify drinking water, cook food, dry clothing, and signal for help. Know that you can guild a fire before heading into the wilds. (February 01, p.16)

Mr. Robert Smith, of Catskill, NY, writes: Drop your only matches in the river? If you remember to carry some fine-grade steel wool along with your flashlight, you needn't worry. Simply unscrew the flashlight cap, and place one end of a small clump of the steel wool to the top of the positive battery post and on the other to the negative contact strip (make sure the switch is on). With a Mag-Lite, unscrew the bulb, turn the light on, and touch the steel wool to the bulb socket. A spark will appear on the wool. Slowly blow on it until it begins to flame. Carefully place the lit wool on a pile of kindling, and start your fire as usual. (June 01, p. 53)

Eat the foods you like. Real eggs can be carried in plastic cartons. Mini drip filters keep the coffee addicts happy. Use insulated plastic mugs with snap-on lids. They prevent spills in the tent, keep beverages hot, and, unlike classic tin cups, allow people to drink without scalding their lips. In sandy or sloppy conditions improve the neatness of mealtimes by cooking on a ground cloth.

No matter which pack you own, load it meticulously. Place light objects, like the sleeping bag and sleeping pad, at the bottom and outer side of the pack. Put heavy objects—fuel canisters, water bottles, food bag—close to your back and at the top inner portion of the pack so that their weight bears straight down upon your hips. Raingear and frequently-used clothing such as jacket, hat, and gloves go in the top of pack toward its outer side. Tents can be placed horizontally under the top flap of the pack and close to the shoulders. Guns and fishing rods can be strapped on vertically along the sides. (September 95, p.39)

FIRE! HOW TO CHEAT AT BUILDING ONE.

Have a kit assembled instead of relying on nature, which can be all the more stressful and time consuming in your efforts to get warm. Instead, assemble a kit to fit in your pack or pocket. The kit, which should fit inside a gallon-size resealable bag should include:

• A waterproof plastic safe or spare sulfur-tipped wooden matches. You could include a butane lighter, but never depend on it as the sole means of fire production.

• A commercial carbon-stick firestarting device, such as the Metal Match or Gerbers Strike Force for backup.

• Three or four one- or two-inch candle stubs, either home cut or purchased commercially. (Use these to ignite reluctant kindling in unfavorable fire-making conditions.)

• One or two hand-warmer packets. Numb fingers can limit your ability to initiate a flame. (February 01, p. 16)

Be a smart camper. It's nice to have some running water handy, but avoid camping too close to the water. Quiet eddies usually harbor insects galore, which invite themselves to your camp once they find out you are nearby. Camp in an open area so you can see bears coming and more easily scare them off from a distance. Keep a clean camp, and keep food well up off the ground, at least 10 feet high and five feet out from the tree trunk. Look uphill for torn-up trees and brush, which can indicate landslides. (September 95, p.70)

Seal the seams of the tent according to the manufacturer's instructions. If you don't, it will leak. Period.

Plants or fruits that wildlife eat are not necessarily safe for human consumption. Hundreds of cultivated and wild plants contain substances highly toxic to man. For example, the purple berries of pokeweed are eaten with impunity by wild birds and chickens, but the berry and its seeds contain substances that can be fatal.

Pine needles of any species can be steeped in hot water to make a tea rich in vitamin C. The fresh shoots of young pine saplings can be eaten raw, but are better if boiled to near transparency. (July 95, p.72)

"The first merit-badge book was wolf, then bear. I thought 'wolf, bear, this is pretty slow progression. At this rate we'll never get to women.'"

—Jerry Seinfeld, on being a Cub Scout, 1993. (November 94, p.55)

Sportsmen, add Super Glue to your survival kits. This adhesive proves to be a surefire method to close cuts and stop the bleeding. Although Super Glue has limited applicability, it can successfully stitch up minor lacerations until a doctor's visit is made.

When an eyeball is cut or impaled, there is little you can or should do in the field. The best recourse, generally, is to patch the eye (if patching is possible without causing further pain or injury) and evacuate immediately to a hospital.

If you hooked your best friend, or yourself for that matter, forget about the conventional method of pushing the hook through and clipping the barb. It's a painful method creating more tissue damage than necessary. Instead proceed as follows: 1. Cut a two-foot length of line or leader, preferably 12-pound test or greater. 2. Loop the line around the inside bend of the hook and grasp securely. 3. While pushing downward on the eye of the hook, give a quick firm jerk on the line, with the force directed away from the eye and parallel to the skin. 4. Note the look of amazement on your friends' faces and continue fishing. (June 01, p. 36)

Unfortunately, fishing improves when river flows increase, but your safety doesn't. Safety is critical for anglers who wade dam tailwaters. Water rises dangerously fast when generators come online or floodwaters must be released. Gauge the flow against immovable boulders or trees, note increased vegetation floating downstream, and listen for changes in the river's noise level. (June 01, p. 53)

If someone throws you a rope in fast water, grasp it tightly but never wrap it around your wrist and never tie it to yourself. Tension against the rope (for instance, if it gets caught on an obstacle) could pull you under. You must always be able to instantly let go of the rope, which can quickly change from an instrument of rescue to a cause of death. (April 96, p. 31)

It should be obvious that if you are wearing a PFD (personal flotation device) when you fall in, your chances of survival go way up, because you can stay afloat without expending energy. This is especially important in frigid water, where shock, unconsciousness and hypothermia are immediate dangers. A good PFD will keep your head above the water, even if you black out, or if you're knocked unconscious while falling in. (June 93, p. 36)

Your eyes could be suffocating. That's what happens when you wear contact lenses while hiking, camping, fishing or hunting at altitudes above 5000 feet. Contacts cover your corneas, restricting your eyes ability to take in enough oxygen in the thinner air of the high country. A sure sign your eyes are suffocating is if you see hazy rings or halos around bright lights. The solution is simple: Take out your contacts for a while and let your corneas drink in as much oxygen as possible. Even the brief respite while cleaning your lenses is good for eyes at high altitudes. (October 97, p.95)

Many hours of daylight and a full moon on the 12th mean you won't have much need for a flashlight in the back country. If the weather is fine, it's also an appropriate time to try those long, difficult routes. (June 95, p. 53)

A chigger is specifically a red mite. They don't suck blood, and the bite itself isn't painful. Instead, they attach themselves to the outer skin with tiny jawlike pincers, secreting an enzyme that dissolves the skin cells into a thick liquid they can then drink. The chemical reaction to the enzyme, not the bite itself, is what causes the itching. If you get chiggers, there isn't much to do about it except scratch. They seek out areas where your clothing fits tightly, and where the skin folds. Although they'll feed on you for only three or four days, the itch from the enzymatic reaction can last for as many as 10 days. (April 96, p. 82)

The first sign of Lyme disease in 60 to 80 percent of the cases is a rash—a reddish blotch or bullseye pattern, often no more than 2½ inches across. If untreated it may in the course of two weeks to a month expand to four times that area. The rash does not always occur at the bite site, often appearing at the armpit, groin or back of the knee. Other early signs include chills, fever and fatigue. If untreated, Lyme may cause long-term problems that can appear months or even years later, including severe headaches, arthritis, nervous-system disorders and heart troubles. (August 96, p. 47)

The myth of removing an embedded tick by touching it with a hot match or by covering it with alcohol or fingernail polish is not advised after further review. Though these methods have long been used, they actually increase the likelihood of infection or transmission of disease, because they cause the tick to disgorge infectious material into the wound. Instead, grab the tick as close as possible to the skin with a pair of tweezers, pulling directly upward with steady, gentle pressure until the tick releases its hold. Twisting or yanking should be avoided. These methods can result in broken off mouthparts embedded in the skin. Once the tick is removed, clean the site with a mild disinfectant. (June 01, p. 16)

Mosquitoes are more attracted to blue than any other color. (March 96, p.54)

WEATHER WISE ANIMALS:

1. If squirrels are laying in large stores of nuts, or if a turkey's feathers are unusually thick by Thanksgiving, expect a hard winter. 2. If gulls stay on the beach, fishermen should do the same. 3. When dew is on the grass, rain will come to pass; when grass is dry at night, look for rain before the light. 4. When the rooster crows late at night, he tells you that a rain's in sight. 5. The wider the black bands on a woolly bear caterpillar, the harsher the winter will be.

Should you ever come in contact with a bear, your actions can determine the outcome. Obviously, it is a mistake to run, but, less obviously, it's a mistake to play dead too soon. Dozens of case histories have people dropping to the dirt as soon as the bear comes near, thereby precipitating an avoidable charge. Stand still. Don't move, even if the bear charges.

A charge is not an attack until the bear touches you, and bears will often stop short or turn aside before making contact. In a standoff, do not look the bear in the eye—this may be perceived as aggression on your part. Instead, look off, down or to the side, 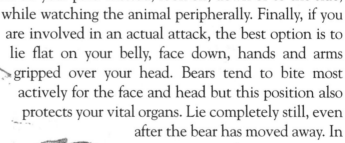 while watching the animal peripherally. Finally, if you are involved in an actual attack, the best option is to lie flat on your belly, face down, hands and arms gripped over your head. Bears tend to bite most actively for the face and head but this position also protects your vital organs. Lie completely still, even after the bear has moved away. In many case histories, retreating bears returned for a second mauling when the victims stirred or yelled out to soon.

When floating a river, always keep on board a watertight bag packed with a complete dry change of clothes, butane lighter, flashlight, Space Blanket, water and food. You probably won't need it, but if you take a spill or have an accident, an emergency kit like this can be a lifesaver. (Summer 97, p.83)

WHEN YOU'RE LOST, S.T.O.P.

S = Stop. If you think you're lost, or even mildly turned around, stop! Don't keep walking around fumbling forward, hoping everything will suddenly look familiar. Sit down, get comfortable, and rest.

T = Think. Don't panic. The thought of being lost, the embarrassment, and ridicule that is sure to follow a mishap are sure to jump into thoughts of failure. Sit down, take a few calming breaths, and maybe a drink of water, a bite to eat if you have food. This provides a conscious and unconscious reassurance that you are still in control.

O = Orient. Get back to recognizable ground. Ask yourself: Where are you in relation to landmarks you might recognize? Which fork or trail or detour did you take? How long have you been off course or uncertain? Can you backtrack with reasonable certainty to the last familiar point? Stay calm and answer these questions.

P = Plan. So now you have oriented, and face the question of whether or not to find your way back, or stay put. In both situations there have been case histories of victims, so the decision could be monumental in your future safety.

Some hay fever sufferers claim to have eliminated symptoms forever by ingesting regular doses of wildflower honey during the off-season. The therapy makes sense. By exposing your sensitive immune system every day to the substances it's sensitive to, you build up a tolerance. Others swear by bee pollen, which is more likely than honey to contain the pollen or ragweed that your body finds irritating. This naturopathic approach works on the same principle as the immunotherapy you'd receive at your doctor's office. But allergy specialists warn that if you're allergic to bee stings, don't try bee pollen.

If bitten by the ferocious mosquitoes, chiggers, or fire ants, don't fret. Apply Preparation H instantly and notice the effects. It should relieve the discomfort and the next morning there should be no redness or other indication of the bites.

Sunburn remedy—An old woodsman's trick. Swab white vinegar on the sunburned areas. The pickled-egg smell will last about an hour or two but the pain will vanish after an evening's rest.

For those who deal with stuffy noses, watery eyes, and consistent discomfort from hay fever, keep these tips in mind when battling the pollens and mold spores. Avoid vigorous exercise when pollen levels are highest, like on windy days with high temperatures and low humidity. Change your clothes after lengthy outdoor exposure, and take a shower, washing your hair immediately. Pollen's ability to cling to hair, clothing and furniture is tenacious. Avoid wearing contact lenses when you know you'll be exposed to ragweed. Wear protective goggles and a dust mask when gardening or cutting the grass. (September 97, p. 64)

If thick trees or natural windbreaks are scarce, the fastest and most effective way to get out of the elements for the night is to dig a snow trench. In soft snow, use whatever is available to dig out a trench long and wide enough to accommodate your body. Frozen, crusted snow may need to be cut out in blocks using a long knife, ice ax, ski or flat-whittled stick. (Save the blocks to cover the trench later.) Dig 2½ to three feet deep, and make a deeper  sink section at the foot end to receive colder, sinking air. Stamp the floor flat, then cover it with boughs, leaves or bark. Never sleep directly on the snow unless you have no other choice. Cover the trench using snow blocks, a weighted down tarp, branches, or even a cross-hatching of equipment. Though far from idyllic, the trench's insulated, wind-protected interior will be substantially warmer than the raw air above. (November 97, p. 40)

It's important to realize that true frostbite, in which the damage is deeper and more extreme, is not necessarily associated with severe cold. Research shows that most frostbite injuries occur between 0 and 25 degrees F, and are often the result of prolonged exposure. (February 96, p. 40)

Wear proper socks. Socks that arc too thin fail to provide an adequate buffer against the insole and heel leather, while overly thick socks make a tight fit, increasing abrasion. (May 93, pA4)

Sometimes getting warm in the wild is easier than you think. The best of all winter shelters are the ones nature has already configured or half-built. Caves (even small ones), rock coves in open country, arroyos, dry creekbeds and other kinds of hollows can give you a significant head start when building shelter. A rock wall under a low ledge overhang could prove an excellent shelter if you insulate the floor with boughs or leaves and branches, then build a reflector fire. Heat from the fire will reflect off the rock wall, creating an oven effect, with you in the middle.

Conifer Conversions are also excellent sources of shelter in snow country. A snug, dry cave can be made by digging into the leeward base of a snow covered spruce. A small fire near the entrance will provide additional warmth. In deep snow regions, thick conifers may form a snowless pit around the base of their trunks. Sometimes it takes only a small bit of burrowing through surface snow to break through to the needle-covered inner hollow, which can provide life-saving shelter from wind or storm. The floor can be further insulated with broken, layered boughs, while the lower tree branches make the roof. This must be a fireless shelter, though if you have a candle you can use it for both light and warmth.

A single candle flame can raise the temperature of a well-made snow shelter from 10 degrees to 30 degrees F. The fallen or cut tree shelter is useful in situations where the snow is not very deep. Cut or break away enough boughs to create a small, body-sized hollow within the tree. Layer the cut boughs to form a floor or a bed. Build a reflector fire near the opening for more heat.

Fremont's Disastrous Fourth Expedition

By Micajah McGehee

Colonel John Charles Fremont, guided by celebrated frontiersman Kit Carson, made three expeditions across the American west in the 1840s. The reports he sent back did much to spur westward expansion and made him one of the most famous men in 19th century America.

On his fourth expedition, Fremont set out late in the fall of 1848 to find a possible route for the transcontinental railroad through the San Juan Mountains of southern Colorado. He assumed that if he could find a route easy enough for his party of thirty-three men to negotiate in winter, the railroad engineers would have little trouble following. He hired the famous mountain man "Old" Bill Williams to lead the party after several other guides refused due to their knowledge of the rugged mountains and the early winter weather that year.

Fremont himself wrote very little about the disaster that followed, despite penning voluminous accounts of all his other exploits. Several survivors kept diaries on the journey, however; this one, by Micajah McGehee, is one of the best.

WE ENTERED THE MOUNTAINS ON FOOT and the snow rapidly deepened and we continued on foot, packing our saddle mules with corn to sustain the animals. We traveled on, laboring

45

through the deep snow upon the rugged mountain range, passing through successively what are called White Mountain Valley and Wet Mountain Valley, into Grand River Valley. The cold was intense and storms would frequently compel us to lie in camp, from the impossibility of forcing the mules against them, and the certainty of freezing if we attempted to proceed, for a number of the men were frozen in their limbs in such attempts before we could go a mile from camp. The animals became exhausted and poverty stricken from the inclemency of the weather, and the want of food, what little grass there had been being all buried in the snow.

Times grew worse and worse as we proceeded. The mules gave out, one by one and dropped down in the trail, and their packs were placed upon the saddle mules. The cold became more and more intense even to such a degree that the thermometer would not indicate the temperature, it being many degrees below zero and the mercury sinking entirely into the bulb.

Crossing what we called the Sand Hills, and those bleak, bald ridges between the White Mountain and Wet Mountain Valleys, the very aspect of the men was chilling. The breath would freeze upon their faces and their lips be so stiff from the ice that it was almost impossible to speak, their eyelids in a similar condition from the freezing of the water which the cold wind would force from them, the ice standing on their lashes. Long icicles hung down from the nostrils, and the long beard and the hair stood out white and stiff with the frost, each hair standing to itself.

The aspect of the mules was suited to that of the men; their eyelashes and the long beards about their mouths stood like icicles and their breath passing back settled upon their breast and sides until they were perfectly white with frost, and the snow would clog upon their fetlocks and under their hoofs until it formed a ball six inches long, making them appear as though they were walking on stilts. With the deep snow around us, and the pendent frost upon the leafless trees nature and ourselves presented a very compatible picture. Two trappers, Old Bill informed us, were frozen to death here the year previous.

We came through Robideau's Pass, the passage of which was exceedingly difficult, for it was completely filled with the fallen timber prostrated by some previous year's hurricane, amongst which the snow lay deep, and the mules were continually stumbling and falling over these and down the rocky slants. Emerging from this and camping near its extremity, the Colonel, with several others, rode back to examine another pass, and soon returned, one or two with frozen feet.

We descended into Grand River Valley. The snow lay deep as elsewhere and there was no sign of vegetation. One broad, white, dreary looking, plain lay before us, bounded by white mountains. High, precipitous, and frozen mountains were behind us, and this broad dreary plain lay between us and the Rio Grande fifty miles ahead of us. So we entered with the determination of getting through it as quickly as possible. We traveled late and camped in the middle of it, without any shelter from the winds, and with no fuel but some wild sage, a small shrub which grew sparsely around. The cold was intense, the thermometer at night standing at 17 degrees below zero, and it was so cold during the day that Ducatel, a young fellow in the company, came very near freezing to death.

By collecting a quantity of the sage, we made sufficient fires to cook, or rather half cook, our suppers of deer meat, five of these animals having been killed this evening by two of the men, and, bolting down the half-cooked meat, we quickly turned into our blankets in order to keep somewhat warm and for protection against the driving snow for, since leaving the states we had scarcely ever stretched tents. In the night, as ill luck would have it, our mules, poor creatures, which stood shivering in the cold with bowed backs and drooping heads, suffering from their exposed situation and half starved, being now reduced to a pint of corn twice a day, and having no other resource for food, broke loose from their weak fastenings of sage bushes and started off *en masse* on the back trail in order to obtain the shelter of the mountains we had left the day before or to find some shrubbery they could eat. As soon as it was ascertained that they were gone, in the middle of the night, we had to rise from our beds, lifting half a foot of snow with our top blankets, and strike out in pursuit of them through the severe cold.

We overtook them several miles from camp and, taking them back, made them secure. But we rested little the balance of the night.

The next day we reached the Rio Grande del Norte, which we found frozen over, and camped in the river bottom, thickly timbered with cottonwood and willow. We had considerable difficulty in crossing the river, the mules slipping upon the ice and falling or breaking through in places, when we would have to raise them to their feet or draw them over the ice. We found some game, deer and elk, in the river bottom, of which we killed a few. The snow was deeper along here than we had seen it anywhere previously, and our camps, pitched upon it, presented a dreary prospect.

After traveling the whole day in a perfect storm of snow, towards night we would camp in the midst of it and, unpacking our mules, turn them loose to wander about and browse upon whatever shrubs or ends of twigs might chance to remain uncovered. Then digging out of the snow the fallen limbs of the dead fallen timber which lay buried beneath it, the ends here and there projecting out, we would build our fires in amongst the snow upon the top of which we slept at night, rolled in our blankets, first going through the process of thawing it from our feet where it would gather and become clogged while wading through the deep snow after our mules in order to feed and blanket them as night approached.

Here I first got my feet frozen as did several others, the result, in part, of wearing boots, for which I quickly substituted moccasins with blanket wrappers which are much warmer than socks. These are worn altogether by the mountain men whom experience has taught their advantages. They allow a freer exercise and consequently a more rapid circulation and greater warmth than is the case in wearing boots. Moccasins with blanket wrappers for the feet and with leggings of the same material afford the best protection for the lower extremities against severe cold.

Continuing up the river two or three days, we again entered the mountains which soon assumed a very rugged character, and we continued ascending toward the Sierra Madre. Nature here presents herself with all her features prominent and strongly marked, her figures bold and colossal. Peaks, crags, and gorges, of Alpine boldness, confronted us on all sides with their rocky barriers. Our progress became slow and laborious. Our track lay through deep mountain gorges, amid towering precipices and beetling crags, and along steep declivities where, at any other season it would be next to impossible to travel, but where now the deep snows afforded a secure foothold.

In making the ascent of some of these precipitous mountain sides, now and then a mule would lose his footing and go tumbling and rolling many feet down with his pack until he lodged among the rocks below. My saddle mule took one of these tumbles. Losing her foothold, she got her rope hitched upon a large log which lay loosely balanced upon the rocks and knocking me down and jerking the log clear over my head they went tumbling down together. But fortunately no one was hurt.

A great obstacle to our progress were the rapid, rough-bottomed, but boggy streams that we had frequently to encounter in the narrow and deep ravines, where the mules would get balked, half a dozen at a time with their packs on. Then we had to wade in up to our middle amongst the floating ice in the freezing water to help them out.

The farther we went the more obstacles we had to encounter, and difficulties beset us so thick and fast on every hand as we advanced that they seemed threatening to thwart our expedition; but it was determined to continue as long as one chance remained.

Our position assumed a threatening aspect. The snow became deeper daily and to advance was but adding dangers to difficulties. About one-third of the men were already frost-bitten more or less; some of the mules would freeze to death every night, and every day as many more would give out from exhaustion and be left on the trail, and it seemed like combatting fate to attempt to proceed, but we were bent on our course and we continued to advance.

At one time, men were sent ahead to report the prospect; they returned, stating that grass appeared in the distance before them and supposed the snow was abating, but, on coming up, what they saw proved to be the tops of bushes six feet high, projecting above the snow, nor did anything appear upon which the animals could subsist. The corn we had packed along for them was already consumed.

Sometimes we would attempt to move on and the severity of the weather would force us back into camp. In one of these attempts, before we could beat our way half a mile against the tempest, our guide, Old Bill Williams, had nearly frozen; he dropped down upon his mule in a stupor and was nearly senseless when we got into camp. A number of the men came in with their noses, ears, faces, fingers, and feet, partially frozen, and one or two of the mules dropped down and froze to death under their packs.

These times were tough. Poor mules! It was pitiable to see them; they would roam about all night generally on account of their extreme weakness, following back the path of the previous day, pawing in the snow three or four feet deep for some sign of vegetation to keep them alive. They would fall down every fifty yards under their packs and we would have to unpack them and lift them up, and that with fingers frozen and lacerated by the cold. Finally the mules began eating the ropes and rawhide lariats with which they were tied, until there were no more left in camp to tie them with, then they ate the blankets which we tied over them at night, then came in camp and ate the pads and rigging off the pack-saddles, and ate each others tails and manes entirely bare, even into the flesh, and would come to us while sleeping and begin to eat the blankets off us; would tumble into our fires over the cooking utensils, and even stick their noses into the kettles for something to eat. But, poor things, little relief could we afford them; for, though they suffered much, we were in no better condition. Our provisions were nearly exhausted, and we were more or less frozen.

Finally, on the 17th of December, after frequent ineffectual attempts, we found that we could force our way no further. By our utmost endeavors with mauls and spades, we could make but half a mile or a mile per day. The cold became more severe and storms constant so that nothing was visible at times through the thick driving snow. For days in succession, we would labor to beat a trail a few hundred yards in length, but the next day the storm would leave no trace of the previous day's work.

When we built our camp fires, deep pits were formed by the melting of the snow, completely concealing the different messes from each other. Down in these holes we slept, spreading our blankets upon the snow; every morning crawling out from under a deep covering of snow which had fallen upon us during the night. The strong pine smoke, for here there was no other timber but pine, together with the reflection from the snow, so affected our sight that at times we could scarcely see a particle, and the snow drifted over us continually, driven about by the violence of the chill blasts that swept over the mountains constantly.

Besides ourselves and ours, no vestige of animal life appeared here in this lofty and dreary solitude; not even the ravens uttered their hoarse cry, nor the wolves their hollow and dismal howl, wonted visitants of unfrequented places. The mules stood huddled together on the mountain, after vainly searching for grass, their ears frozen and their limbs cracked and bleeding from cold; they would drop down and die, one by one, and, in a single night, nearly the entire band of over one hundred mules had frozen to death.

After remaining in this condition for five days without being able to move camp, with no prospect of better things, our provisions being almost entirely gone and the mules having nearly all perished, compelled to abandon our present course, the Colonel determined to endeavor as quickly as possible to return by a different direction to the Rio Grande. There we had left game upon which we could subsist until a party, to be previously dispatched, should return with relief; and whence, having obtained a fresh supply of animals, we could, crossing the mountains by a different direction, still pursue a westerly course on the 38th degree.

So, on the 22nd of December, we commenced our move crossing over the bleak mountain thickly strewn with the frozen mules, and packing our baggage with us. We were more than a week moving our camp and equipage over the top of this mountain (a distance of two miles only from our first camp), owing to the intensity of the weather. The same day that we began to move, our provisions being all consumed except a small portion of macaroni and sugar, reserved against hard times, we commenced eating the carcasses of the frozen mules, for it was hoped that we might save the few that yet lived; but it was impossible, and we began to kill and eat the surviving ones. In butchering them, some of the men would return to camp with fingers perfectly hard frozen, such was the degree of cold. Capt. Cathcart said: "Who'd 'a thought it? A Captain in the 11th Prince Albert's Hussars eating mulemeat and packing his baggage amongst the snows of the Rocky Mountains!"

On Christmas Day, the Colonel dispatched a party of four men, King, Creutzfeldt, Breckenridge, and Bill Williams, to proceed down the Rio del Norte with all possible speed to Albequeque where they were to procure provisions and mules to relieve us. He allowed them sixteen days to go and return. We made our Christmas and New Year's dinner on mule meat, not the fattest either as may be judged, and continued to feed upon it while it was within reach, for we had undertaken to pack all our baggage, saddles, pack-saddles, etc., on our backs through the deep snow to the river, where we would be able to recover them. We made a sledge for this purpose, but it did not work well and we abandoned it.

Our way to the river was very rough, passing over rugged and precipitous mountain spurs, difficult of passage, and deep ravines with rapid streams frozen over in which the water was pitching and roaring beneath us as we crossed. We would move camp three or four miles at a time, then packing all the baggage down we would move again in the same way; on an average, at our best, scarcely making a mile per day, for wading through the deep snow was very laborious. It would bear us up for two or three steps with our load but, at the next step, we would break through and go in waist deep when we would have to scramble out the best way we could, and try it again. We took advantage of every steep descent and, fixing our packs in the parfleches so that they would slide, we would give them a start and they would go sliding and bounding along down, fifty or a hundred yards at a stretch, when, acquiring a tremendous momentum, they would sometimes bolt out and, plunging ten or fifteen feet, come with great violence against a tree or rock which would stop their progress. Occasionally they would take a fellow before them about the heels and knocking his feet from under him away they would all go together.

But our labor became very exhausting, for we were now on short allowance, and our starvation also ill fitted us to endure the cold. On our way the last provision was issued out, a little macaroni and sugar, and we began eating the rawhide tugropes and parfleches, cutting it in strips and boiling it to a sort of glue, or burning it on the coals until it was soft enough to bite.

Times were getting squally. Between the last camps over a bleak and barren stretch of seven miles before reaching the river, the cold was unusually severe and perfectly unbearable, storms prevailing continually, which rendered it almost impossible for us to make the distance across in a single day, being compelled frequently to take refuge under the shelter of the rocks, making a fire of what sticks or other material we could find to keep from freezing.

In crossing this stretch ere reaching the river, one of the party, Proue, had frozen to death beside the trail; we passed and repassed his lifeless body, not daring to stop long enough in this intense cold to perform the useless rites of burial.

One day I started across this stretch, determined to go on to the river that night or freeze. Andrews started with me but, before we could get half way across, he became exhausted and lay down upon the snow, declaring that he could go no further, and that he would freeze to death if he attempted it. I tried to urge him on, but he could not go and I could not leave him; so, proceeding a short distance, I got him into a cave of the rock, which afforded a shelter against the severity of the storm; then, climbing among the rocks, I ascended to the top of the mountain where the wind was blowing such a perfect hurricane that I would have to lie flat down, at times, to keep from being swept off. Taking advantage of the intervals between the gusts of wind, I rolled down some of the pinòn logs which lay upon the mountainside, pitching them over the crags below and, descending to the cave, struck a fire.

By this time, two others, Capt. Cathcart and R. Kern, arrived to take shelter from the storm. They had not a thing to eat, and we had our last portion; in the extremity of our starvation we had the day before divided out the last morsel which remained of anything to eat, and the share that fell to each man was a cupful of boiled macaroni and a cup of sugar. This we had with us and we offered to share it with them, but, *miserabile vieu,* Andrews, in trying to warm it, by an unlucky move, upset it into the fire; thus went the last mouthful that we had to eat on earth, and we half starved.

The storm continued to rage with such violence that we could not leave, and here it kept us for two whole days. In looking around, I found a small roll of rawhide snowshoe strings which had been left by one of the men. These we cut in pieces and boiled them. I also found some dry bones in an old wolf den among the rocks; how many years they had been lying there, I will not undertake to say, but these we pounded to pieces between rocks and boiled them with the strings and, upon this mess, we four lived for two days. A number of others on their way had been forced, like us, to take shelter here and there among the rocks from the storm.

We reached the river. No game was there; the hope upon which we had depended was disappointed; the deer and elk had been driven off by the deep snow. For days we had been anxiously looking for the return of King's party with relief. The time allotted him had already expired and day after day passed by, but no prospect of relief came and we concluded that either the party had been attacked by Indians and had all been killed, or they had lost their way and perished.

The time allowed for King's return having passed (January 9), the Colonel, who had moved down to the river before us, waited two days longer, and then (January 11), taking just enough provision before it was all exhausted to do them down the river, himself started off with Mr. Preuss, Godey, Theodore (Godey's nephew) and Sanders, the Colonel's servant man, intending to find out what had become of the party and hasten them back; or, if our fears concerning them proved true, to push on himself to the nearest settlement and send relief.

He left an order that we scarce knew how to interpret, to the effect that we must finish packing the baggage to the river and hasten on down as speedily as possible to the Mouth of Rabbit River where we would meet relief, and that if we wished to see him we must be in a hurry as he was going on to California. By this time, being forced to abandon his projected route, he had determined to proceed to California by a Southern route.

Two days after the Colonel left (about January 13), we had all collected on the river. The last of our provisions had been consumed and we had been living for several days upon parfleche. Our condition was perilous in the extreme. Starvation stared us in the face. To remain here longer was certain death. We held a consultation and determined to start down the river the next day, and try and make the best of our way to some settlement where we could get relief, in the meantime keeping as much together as possible, and hunting along as we went, as our only chance of safety.

The two Canadian Frenchmen, Tabeau, or "Sorrell" as we called him, and Moran, did not delay as long as we but, pinched by hunger, had started off the day before.

So, with a handful of sugar to each man, we divided some candles, pieces of rawhide, tugropes and parfleches and, strapping on a blanket apiece, and shouldering our rifles, we started on our gloomy march down the frozen river. Over its congealed surface a sombre shade was cast by the overhanging trees covered with the long white frost which hung like a thick fringe from their barren boughs. Tottering from weakness and some with frozen and bleeding feet, we made slow progress. We kept upon the ice down the middle of the river to get a level track, and to avoid as much as possible the deep snow. Now commenced a train of horrors which it is painful to force the mind to dwell upon, and which memory shrinks from. Before we had proceeded far, Manuel, a California Indian of the Cosumne tribe, who had his feet badly frozen, stopped and begged Mr. Vincenthaler to shoot him and, failing to meet death in this way, turned back to the lodge at the camp we had left, there to await his fate. The same day Wise lay down upon the ice on the river and died; the Indian boys, Joaquin and Gregorio, who came along afterward, having stopped back to get some wood for Manuel, seeing his (Wise's) body, covered it over with brush and snow. That night, Carver, crazed by hunger, raved terribly all night, so that some in the camp with him became alarmed for their safety. He told them, if any would follow him back, he had a plan by which they might live. The next day he wandered off and we never saw him again. The next night "Sorrell," his system wrought upon by hunger, cold and exhaustion, took a violent fit, which lasted upon him for some time; it resulted in an entire prostration of all his faculties. At the same time, he was almost totally snowblind. Speaking to E. Kern of our situation, he said, "Oh, Kern, this is a *mise Dieu* (a visitation from God), and we can't avoid it." Poor fellow, the next day he traveled as long as his strength would allow, and then, telling us we would have to leave him, that he could go no farther, blind with snow, he lay down on the river bank to die. Moran soon joined him and they never came up again.

Late at night we all, arriving one by one, came into a camp together on the river bank. Gloom and despondency were depicted on every face. Our condition had become perfectly desperate. We knew not what to do; the candles and parfleche had kept us alive thus far, but these were gone. Our appearance was desolate as we sat in silence around the fires, in view of a fast approaching death by starvation, while hunger gnawed upon our vitals.

Then Vincenthaler, to whom the Colonel had left the charge of the camp, and whom, for that reason, we had allowed to have the chief direction, spoke up and told us then and there threw up all authority; that he could do nothing and knew not what to advise; that he looked upon our condition as hopeless, but he would suggest as the best advice he could give, that we break up into small parties and, hunting along, make the best of our way down separately, each party making use of all the advantages that might chance to fall in its way, to hasten on down without waiting for the others so that, if any chanced to get through to a settlement, they could forward relief to the others.

Accordingly, the next morning he joined himself with Scott, Martin, Hibbard, Bacon, Ducatel, Rohrer, and the two Indians, Joaquin and Gregorio, who had left the mess that they were in, for fear, as they said, that certain men in it would kill them to eat when it came to the worst.

Ferguson and Beedle went together; and the rest of us — the three Kearns, Capt. Cathcart, Capt. Taplin, myself, Stepperfeldt, and Andrews — went together, and we agreed not to leave each other while life lasted. Again we renewed our unsteady course down the river. We traveled hard all day and, late in the evening, weak and worn out, we staggered into a camp near the river side, some coming in far behind the rest. Dr. Kern came up so exhausted that he fell down, almost senseless, and remained in this torpid state a whole day. After awhile Andrews came up; arriving within several hundred yards of camp, he raised a faint call and fell down, completely exhausted and senseless so that two or three of us had to go and pack him in. He never recovered from this exhaustion. Soon Rohrer came up. Vincenthaler's party, to which he belonged, was ahead of us; being too weak to proceed farther, he stopped with us.

Here we remained, determined, as we had promised, not to leave any while they lived. So we commenced hunting around, all that had strength and sight sufficient to do so, for most of us were so completely snowblind that we could not see to shoot. After long and frequent hunts, two prairie chickens or grouse were killed. These we divided with scrupulous exactness among the nine of us, dividing the entrails and all that appertained to them, even to the pin feathers. Taplin found part of a dead wolf upon the river and brought it in. All one side and the entrails had been eaten away, but we divided the skin and roasted it, hair and all, for one meal, drank the meagre broth for another, and then ate the meat and even devoured the bones. This was the last we got.

Day after day we stayed here but no game came near. Occasionally we could hear the distant, dismal howl of a wolf weary with waiting for its work, but none came near, and, at distant intervals, a raven would go screaming by, beyond our reach, but never stopping within sight. We found a handful or two of rosebuds along the river which we divided and ate, and Dr. Kern found a few small bugs upon the water where the ice was broken and ate them. We had already devoured our moccasin soles, and a small sack made of smoked lodge skin. We dug in the ground beneath the snow with our knives for roots, but it was a useless labor.

We became weaker daily, and to walk thirty steps once a day after some dry cottonwood sticks to keep up our fire fatigued us greatly. Our strength was rapidly failing. Andrews died in the course of the night as he lay by our side, after lingering out several days and, the next day, Rohrer was nearly gone, talking wildly, a fearful expression of despair resting upon his countenance. The mention of his family at home had served to rouse him and keep him going longer than his strength would otherwise have born him up; but now it was too late; his case was over. Taking from Andrews' pocket a small gilt-embossed Bible, carefully preserved, which we intended, in case any of us lived to get through, to hand over as a memento to his friends, we laid his body to one side and covered it with a blanket; then we sat down, waiting until Rohrer should die, intending (as soon as the breath had left his body), to commence another move down the river, continuing by slow degrees until our powers should entirely fail.

As we sat waiting, _____ came over to the fire where

58

Taplin, I, and Stepperfeldt were sitting and, in a sad tone, said: "Men, I have come to make a proposition. I don't know how you will take it. It is a horrid one. We are starving. In two or three days more, except something is done, we will all be dead. Here lies a mass of useless flesh, from which the life has departed, which, as soon as we leave, will be the prey of wild beasts. There is enough to keep us all alive. It is nothing but our prejudices that causes us to look upon human flesh as anything more than any other flesh. Now, I propose that, instead of leaving it to become food for wolves, we make use of it to save human life. It is horrid, I know, but I will undertake to do the butchery, as you may call it, and you need have nothing to do with that part; you need not even see it done. Do you agree to my proposition?"

All sat in silence, then several of us objected, and I spoke up and said: "For my part, I have no conscientious scruples against such a procedure. I know that early prejudice and conventional opinion founded on prejudice are at the bottom of our objections to it, but these exist, and this is a horrid proposition to entertain. I fully appreciate our situation, but I think that by making up our minds to it and remaining quiet we can yet hold out three days longer, by which time, after finding that we cannot possibly bear up longer, there will then be time enough to think of adopting so horrible alternative; then, if I do not approve, I will not censure it."

"And by that time," he said, "we will be too weak and too far gone ever to recover and we will all starve to death here in a mass. You see what they have come to and you see what you will come to."

"I can't help it," I said, "I am determined to risk it at the peril of my life," and, so saying, I walked over to the other fire. They talked about it a few minutes but were unwilling to do such a thing unless all did, and so we all waited together. We remained around the fire, stirring as little as possible and firing signal guns at frequent intervals during the day. Rohrer died. Two days passed and no relief came. Several times we imagined we heard an answer to our signal and would rise up to listen, but being as often disappointed we had ceased to notice.

The morning of the third day (January 25) arrived and was far advanced toward midday, and we sat in the deepest gloom. Suddenly we thought we heard a call.

"Hush!" said one, and we all listened intently.

Another call! "Relief, by God!" exclaimed one of the men, and we all started to our feet.

Relief it was, sure enough, for directly we spied Godey riding toward us, followed by a Mexican. We were all so snowblind that we took him to be the Colonel until he came up and some saluted him as the Colonel. We shook him by the hand heartily. Dismounting, he quickly distributed several loaves among as, with commendable forethought giving us but a small piece at first, and making us wait until the Spaniard could boil some for us, or prepare some "tole" (boiled cornmeal), which he quickly made and this we more quickly devoured. It required considerable persuasion to prevent us from killing the old horse which the Spaniard had, in order to eat it; but Godey informed us there were two colts in the camp below, which, if we would wait, we might have. This was the 25th of January. There were men in the party who did not escape the horrible fate which came so near being ours.

Godey with the Colonel and the rest that were with them, after leaving the party, traveling on as rapidly as possible down the river, came upon two Indians with several old horses, and engaged them to pilot them in; going on they had overtaken King's party, who, leaving the river, had undertaken to strike across the country to Abacue, but becoming involved in the deep snow, their provisions being exhausted, they having eaten their knife scabbards and tried to eat their boots, and with no fuel, being compelled to lie out night after night, without fire, upon the barren plain, until they were more or less frozen from their hips down, had returned to the river, where King died; here the Colonel's party found them in a weak and emaciated condition, and nearly dead, with intellect shaken and scarcely any hearing, sight, or sense left, and half deranged and nearly sightless they took them along upon the Indian horses into the little outer settlement of the Rio Colorado.

Here quickly obtaining what provisions he could, and hiring several Spaniards with mules, Godey set out as speedily as possible up the river. On his way he fell in with two other Mexicans, who, with mules loaded with bread and flour and cornmeal, were going out to trade with the Utah Indians. These he pressed into service with their cargoes, and, hastening on, traveling late and early, he met Vincenthaler's party about 20 miles below us, who had lived by killing a raven, hawk, or prairie chicken occasionally that they had the good luck to meet with; also they had eaten part of a dead horse they found. But two of their number were missing from among them. They had agreed among themselves that, when one became so exhausted that he could not travel, the rest should not wait for him. Hibbard had been first left, and soon after him Scott. Leaving most of the animals and provisions at Vincenthaler's camp, Godey proceeded rapidly up. He found Scott sitting in a listless manner by a fire he had just kindled, his head resting upon his hands, almost totally snowblind. Having strengthened him with food, Godey furnished him a horse and sent a Mexican with him to the camp below; then, proceeding on, he came to Hibbard, who had just died, his body yet warm. Failing in his attempt to restore him, he kept on.

Taking across a short bend in the river, he passed entirely by us without knowing it and found Ferguson a short distance above us. Beedle was dead, and his body was lying near by. Ferguson informed Godey that we were below him, and, coming down with him, he found us.

Leaving us and taking with him several Spaniards with pack-mules, he followed up along our track, which was marked by the bodies of the dead as they had perished day by day, and now were lying the prey of wolves and ravens; the deep and gloomy silence of their solitude only broken by the snarls and yells of packs of wolves, quarreling over their remains. He found the bodies of "Sorrell" and Moran together. Friends in life they proved friends in death. "Sorrel" was lying prostrate on the snow and Moran apparently, after having tried to strike a fire, had dropped his head upon the log against which he was sitting and expired by his side.

Godey found the Indian, Manuel, in the lodge, still alive, and brought him down. Manuel afterward stated that Carver came up to the lodge with a piece of meat which he said was part of a deer he had killed, and that he undertook to go to the previous camp seven miles back for something and had frozen to death. Godey attempted to go back to this camp after some valuables of which we had made a *cache* in the snow before leaving, but two of the mules perished in the cold in the attempt, and he abandoned it and packed down only the lodge and its contents.

At the same time that Godey left us we had sent the Mexican to Vincenthaler's camp for animals to take us down, for we were wholly unable to walk. He returned with them the next day. Tying our blankets on for saddles and rigging rope stirrups, we were lifted (for we could not lift even our skeleton frames) upon as poor looking animals as were ever known to live on nothing, and after a two days journey, which, though the ride was almost killing, was the most welcome horseback excursion we had ever taken, reached the camp 20 miles below.

We were pretty looking objects about then; lank, thin vis-aged, and eyes sunken, our hair and beard long, tangled and knotty, and our faces black with pine smoke which had not been washed off for two months, we resembled more the Spirits of Darkness, or, if anything mortal, a set of banditti, than anything else. Here we fell to eating enormously, and it required the exercise of all our self restraint to prevent plenty now from being as hurtful to us as want had been before. The abundance of food, when there had just been such a lack, made us all sick and kept us sick for some days, but that could not stop us. Our appetite was unbounded and we were eating constantly, at all hours of the day, and through the night. We had such a craving for meat of some kind that we killed two well grown colts and ate them. We were even more ravenous than the ravens themselves, which, now that we did not need them, came crowding round with hawks and wolves. We killed and devoured some of all these.

It was curious to hear different men tell of the workings of their minds when they were starving. Some were constantly dreaming or imagining that they saw before them a bountiful feast, and would make selections of different dishes. Others engaged their minds with other thoughts. For my part, I kept my mind amused by entering continually into all the minutiae of farming or some other systematic business which would keep up a train of thought, or by working a mental solution of mathematical problems, bringing in review the rudiments of some science, or by laying out plans for the future, all having a connection with home and after life. So, in this way, never allowing myself to think upon the hopelessness of our condition, yet always keeping my eyes open to every chance, I kept hope alive and never once suffered myself to despond, and to this course I greatly attribute my support for there were stronger men who, doubtless by worrying themselves, hastened their death.

Ten out of our party of thirty-three that entered the mountains had perished, and several days more would have finished the balance.

Shock victims usually have one or more of these symptoms: 1. Pale, cool, clammy skin. 2. Anxiety and restlessness. 3. Rapid and/or weak pulse. 4. Shallow and/or rapid breathing. 5. Dilated pupils. 6. Nausea and thirst. (May 97, p.61)

BASIC TREATMENT FOR SHOCK:

1. Fluids—consider if appropriate.
2. Elevate legs 8 to 10 inches.
3. Remove wet clothes (if applicable).
4. Lie person flat on the ground on a soft surface and put a blanket or sleeping bad over them immediately.
5. Maintain temperature within normal limits and insulate if necessary.
6. Priorities—airway clear? Victim breathing? Pulse O.K.? Spine injured? (May 97, p. 60)

Stave off hypothermia in the first place by eating a full meal before heading out to fish. Take frequent warming breaks around a fire or car heater; by drinking hot, non-alcoholic beverages regularly; by staying dry; and by dressing warmly while also guarding against sweat buildup inside your clothing. Mostly, know when to get off the water. Even great trout fishing isn't worth dying for. (February 01, p. 69)

Canyon safety. It's difficult to get lost in a major canyon: If you know there is a roadhead at its bottom, you just walk downstream. However, topographic maps help enormously in route finding. They can point out side canyons and escape routes (in case of flash floods), and permit travel from canyon to canyon.

Flash floods are the greatest danger in canyons. The sky can be clear above the canyon river in which you're hiking, while rain is falling in distant mountains at its headwaters. A few hours later a wall of water is at your back. Be a diligent student of the weather and don't venture into narrow canyons if it's storming upstream. Know your escape routes, and be conservative when estimating how long it will take to hike through an inescapable gorge. Place camps well above the riverbed.

The second greatest danger in canyons is climbing off the hiking route. Remember, going up slickrock is far easier than going down. Know your cliff-climbing capabilities beforehand: Find a cliff with sand at its bottom, climb up a dozen feet, then try to reverse your route. (May 96, p.42)

If you fall into cold water and are wearing a PFD, assume the HELP (heat escape lessening posture) position: your head above water, arms crossed over your chest and knees drawn up against your arms. HELP cuts your heat loss in half, which means you can stay alive twice as long while waiting for rescue. If other people are in the water with you, and all or most are wearing PFDs, you can group together in what's called the HUDDLE position; jamming together as closely and tightly as possible arms around each other and legs intertwined to block heat loss. When huddled you also are easier to spot by potential rescuers. (June 93, p. 36)

Should you dump in a boat, first get upstream of the craft and stay there so it can't crash into you as you ride the current. In boulder-strewn water, lie on your back with your head pointing upstream and your feet downstream, to fend off upcoming obstructions without endangering your skull. Backstroke vigorously to steer, while keeping your head up to see the best path through trouble and to safety or rescue.

A 35mm film canister can house a tiny first-aid kit that can easily be stashed in a hunting or fishing vest or daypack. Wrap several pills in aluminum foil labeled with masking tape or a label. H=headache, A=antihistamine, S=stomach indigestion, etc. Label the outside of the canister and fill extra space inside with gauze bandages.

Hunting in cold, rainy weather is a test of endurance, especially in terms of keeping one's fingers from getting numb. Once wet, the hunters hands quickly become chilled, making operation of the safety and trigger difficult and possibly dangerous. A pair of long, gauntlet-style rubber gloves, preferably lined, keep hands dry and fingers dexterous. Even dishwashing gloves will do in a pinch. To be most effective, the gloves should be put on before the raingear; the sleeves will then be outside the gloves, preventing water from funneling in.

Food is literally consumable fuel. Simple sugars burn fastest, flaring up like pitch sticks and providing almost no nutritional value. Complex sugars (carbohydrate starches such as those in grains, nuts and vegetables) burn slowly and evenly, supplying sustained energy without sudden bursts and drops. Proteins and saturated fats burn almost reluctantly; they sit heavily in the stomach, do not translate easily into usable energy, and are often stored as body fat for later burning. A chocolate bar, consisting mostly of simple processed sugar, burns in a flash. It provides a burst of calories that are of little nutritional worth. (June 95, p.38)

Don't wait until you're thirsty to drink water. By the time the body feels thirst, it is already two to five percent dehydrated. Urine color is an indication of dehydration. A dark yellow or brownish urine indicates that you need to drink more water.

If you get a blister while walking over rugged terrain, treat it immediately. Drain the blister immediately. First wash the area with alcohol or soap. Next, sterilize a needle by dipping it into alcohol or by holding the needle's tip over a flame for five seconds. Note that the metal will quickly become hot, so if possible hold it with a pair of pliers or other buffer to prevent finger burns. Pierce the blister at its base, where it meets the underlying skin. Direct the needle upward or laterally. This will cause no pain. Press gently around the blister's edge to drain as much fluid out of it as possible. Do not peel off the layer of dead skin—instead, leave it in place to serve as a built-in surface bandage. Dab the blister with antibiotic ointment (such as Polysporin or Bacitracin) and cover the area with moleskin or a 2nd skin moist pad.

Make sure your boots fit right and break them in well before a trip. Keep them firmly laced all the time for maximum foot comfort. (May 93, pA4)

Carry a spare pair of socks in your daypack and change into them during a midday lunch break. This will perk up your feet and help prevent blisters. (June 93, p.67)

Sock Sag. Cold weather sportsmen have struggled since day one with socks that slide downward until they are a sodden, painful wad under the wearer's toes. To keep socks up where they belong, put them on first, then the long underwear. The legs of long johns will provide friction and keep the socks securely up where they belong. (October 93, p.78)

Used in conjunction with a topo map, an altimeter can help pinpoint your location as well as route you to your destination. A unit that measures altitude in 20-foot increments works well for this type of orienteering. (September 93, p.76)

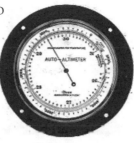

Hunters about to start the season should reacquaint themselves with their compass. Each compass comes from the factory with an instruction sheet. Hunters can use a compass bearing simply to keep track of the direction of travel. (September 93, p.81)

Find an unmistakable geographical line of some kind (a road, railroad track, power line, lakeshore, creek, ridge-line), and establish it as the base from which to begin your path of travel. First, use your compass to confirm the direction of the baseline—say a logging road or creek that runs roughly east to west. Sketch the baseline and its direction in your notebook and note your departure time. If you want to travel north of the baseline, take a northerly but angled off course; a few degrees northwest, for instance—and begin walking. Periodically check your compass to stay on course. When you're ready to return, simply head due south until you hit the baseline. Turn east there, and follow the baseline to your car or camp. (July 95, p.70)

Every survival kit should contain a signalling mirror, an absolutely vital emergency item. Military tests have shown that a mirror, when properly used, can make signal contact as much as 120 miles away (depending on atmospheric conditions). (March 95, p.58)

If you meet a mountain lion when you are hiking, make plenty of noise to reduce the chances of surprising it. Stay calm, talk to it quietly. Do not approach one, especially if it is feeding or with its young. Most will avoid confrontation, so provide an escape. Do all you can to appear larger. Raise your anus, and open your jacket if you have one on. If the lion is behaving aggressively, throw branches or whatever is available at it, without crouching or turning your back. The point is to convince the lion that you may be dangerous. If the lion attacks and you have no gun, fight back. People have fought successfully using rocks, sticks, caps, even bare hands. (July 95, p.54)

When camping, bring extra fuel to heat water, a two-quart pot, and some biodegradable soap. The world looks happier, and packs feel lighter, after even the most minimalist bath.

You can reduce or even escape the effects of poison ivy by bathing within 10 minutes of an exposure, or by rubbing a raw potato over the exposed area.

In the spring the young cattail flower heads and tender stalks can be eaten raw or cooked. Later you can use the pollen to thicken and enrich soups and stews. The roots can be peeled, crushed, and cooked; the smaller, white off-shoots (rootstalks) eaten raw. (July 95, p.72)

The seed heads of thistles can be boiled. With young plants, peel the stalk and eat like celery; use the tender greens and taproots for salad.

The general rule is to let water boil for 5 to 10 minutes, adding one minute for each 1,000 feet of altitude above sea level. But with otherwise pure and cold wilderness water, where the main concern is Giardia or a similar protozoan, you need not boil for this long. Giardia cysts die instantly in water heated to 140° to 160° F. (July 95, p.74)

Insects and other bugs are a good abundant source of nourishment. Grasshoppers, wood grubs, bees and nearly all aquatic insects are edible. So are earthworms, frogs, tadpoles, and minnows. All of these creatures can be safely eaten, but should first be cooked, since some of them could transmit harmful parasites if eaten raw. Boiling, mashing and frying, and roasting (on a stick or atop a flat rock in a fire) all make this food safer and more palatable. (July 95, p.72)

Leaves that curl back and show their undersides indicate the prevailing winds have shifted, which usually means weather is on the way. Lines of birds perched on branches or wires are a clue that the barometer is falling. Low pressure also causes waterfowl to fly low, keeps campfire smoke closer to the ground, and amplifies sounds and odors. Bees swarming actively suggests good weather for at least a day; but their absence may be a hint that precipitation is coming. Symptoms of increasing humidity (such as your own curling hair) point to an approaching storm. A red sky at morning can indeed be a clue to take warning. A red sky at night is a promising sign that the next day will be at least partially fair. (July 95, p.79)

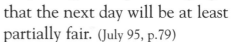

Tips for the cold weather hunter: 1. Get enough to eat and drink. Carry plenty of liquids to replace lost moisture. 2. A calm, pleasant morning can turn into a howling blizzard without warning. Don't get caught unprepared: Hypothermia kills faster than freezing. 3. Don't over-oil your gun; it can cause freeze-up.

Electronic cameras may not work when exposed to frigid conditions. In extreme cold, or in cold and wind, beware of frostbite on exposed skin, particularly on places such as the wrists between gloves and cuffs.

If you are short on water or have run out of it, hole up in the shade during the heat of the day and travel in the comparative coolness of night. Don't travel at all if help can be reasonably expected or signaled in. Studies have shown that if movement is kept to a minimum and proper moisture-conservation measures are practiced, a single quart of water can keep a person alive for as long as two days in 120 degrees F.

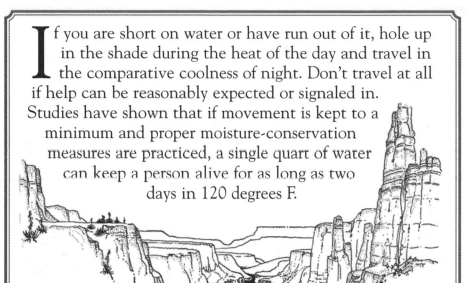

Traps and drops. You may be able to find water by searching in early morning, or after a rainfall. Look for natural pockets, drains and water traps in the desert rock formations. Deep traps can hold water for days after a rain even under scorching conditions. Also look for dew that sometimes forms in early morning on rocks, leaves, tent walls and similar surfaces. Use a piece of absorbent cloth (cotton, for example) to mop up the moisture, which can then be squeezed out and swallowed in droplets.

Look for indicator plants like cottonwoods, sycamores, willows and tamarisk. A line of willows or cottonwoods may indicate where water has been, or where it occurs ephemerally, and is worth checking out—though these species have been seen in places where only a backhoe could reach potable water. (May 95, p.48)

To form a wrap shelter you can use a Space Blanket, which is on hand often, since it fits into pack and even pocket, or a larger canvas or plasticized tarp. For added warmth, beef up the wrap with any kind of natural or artificial insulation (leaves, boughs, dry dirt, newspapers, seat cushion foam— the thicker the better. (December 94, p.36)

In frigid weather, it's important to keep your head covered, even if this means lifting your coat and zipping it over the top of your head (in this case, use other insulation to protect your exposed lower body). Wrap yourself like a cocoon and enjoy a night's rest under the stars.

Emergency blanket for cold feet. First take off all three layers of socks and put on one dry pair. Unfold the emergency blanket and wrap it around your feet so that it comes up to your knees. Be careful that you don't tear it. Now, zip up your sleeping bag and wiggle your feet together for a while. Soon you will feel the warmth come back to them, and chances are you'll have feeling in your toes in no time. (December 93, p.'78)

If your matches get damp, try rubbing them in your hair first before striking. It may be the added measure you need to make them work.
(January 94, p.85)

The Journey Down the Kooskooskee

By Abraham Himmelwright

In September of 1893, three eastern big game hunters, a guide, and a camp cook followed the famous Lolo Trail into remote central Idaho on a hunting expedition. They set up camp along the Lochsa River and hunted deer and elk until the snow began to fall. Unfortunately, the cook fell sick with an illness he had failed to disclose to his companions. The party waited to see if his condition would improve, but soon found themselves completely cut off by deep snow drifts and rugged terrain, unable to use their horses to reach safety.

The only escape route left was through the deep canyons and huge rapids of the river, and the party quickly constructed two log rafts. The story of the journey undertaken by the guide, Spencer, the cook, Colgate, and the three hunters, Carlin, Keeley, and Himmelwright, is taken almost verbatim from Carlin's journal, which Abraham Himmelwright later used in the book he wrote about their adventure.

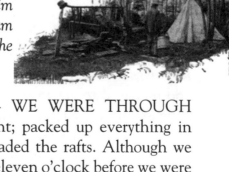

Friday, November 3rd, 1893. — WE WERE THROUGH BREAKFAST shortly after daylight; packed up everything in the most convenient form, and loaded the rafts. Although we hurried as much as possible, it was eleven o'clock before we were ready to start down the river. Old Jerry came down early in the morning to see us off and take some letters which we wished to leave with him, to post to our families in the spring in case we never got out of the mountains. This morning it was cold and cloudy; it began to rain hard about the time we started. It was just 11:30 o'clock when Keeley and Spencer, who manned the lighter raft, shoved off from shore and started down the river. Our raft followed at a distance of about one hundred yards. We had easy water for the first half-mile, when we landed our raft, and John went down around the point to see if Keeley and Spencer got through the first bad rapid all right. He returned in fifteen minutes and reported that the boys had passed through safely, and had landed on the opposite bank below the rapid. We shoved off and stuck on a small rock, but got off in a few minutes. Jerry gave us a parting salute of three shots, and we waved him good-by. When we rounded the point, Spencer motioned us toward his side of the river. We entered the rapid, and just got through the narrow channel without touching the big rocks on either side. Our raft was heavier than theirs and more difficult to land, so we kept right on past them; and rounding the point two hundred yards below, we entered the second bad rapid, of which I had spoken the day before.

This was a difficult place to get through, as the current carried us toward the right bank at the head of the rapid, and the only open channel was along the left-hand side. We had gotten about one-third through, when we struck two large rocks with great force. Not being able to keep the stern from swinging, we were, in a moment, sidewise to the current, jammed against the rocks. The water rushed over the raft and turned its bottom against the rocks, with its side down, and over half the raft was under water. John was thrown off the bow, but he kept hold of his pike-pole, and managed to get in shallow water and thence to the shore. Colgate was sucked under the raft, and was on the point of being swept away, when Abe caught him by the collar of his coat and pulled him on the upper side of the raft. Little Montana [a dog] was drowning, but she was also pulled out high and dry. Spencer and Keeley saw our upset from above the rapid in time to run their raft ashore They came down and tried to wade out to us but could get only a few feet from shore without being washed off their feet. It was impossible to make them understand a word, owing to the roaring of the water, although we were only about twenty yards apart. Finally we managed to make them understand that we wanted them to tie their rope to a tree about one hundred feet above us, and let, their raft down so that they could get over to us and take off our load. It took over an hour to accomplish this. Spencer attended to the rope, and Keeley guided his raft through the rocks along the shore. We sent Colgate, the dogs, and some provisions over in the first load. Abe helped Keeley to land, while I stayed on the raft and got out a second load of blankets, etc. John had worked up the river bank and found a shallow place, where he managed with great difficulty to cross to our side of the river. Colgate and he were cold from the icy water and sleet, which was falling heavily, so Spencer built them a fire. We had just transferred our second load, when our raft, relieved of its weight, rose in the water and partially righted. Abe jumped on, and we loosened it from the rocks and started down the river. We got through the rapid without any further mishap, but could not make a landing below. My pike-pole was jammed in the rocks in the river bottom and jerked out of my hands, and we were carried down for half a mile, when we managed to run fast on a bunch of small rocks in shallow water near the shore, which prevented us from being carried into the rapid below. Wading ashore, we made the raft fast to a root with a rope and "struck out" for camp. We all made as comfortable a camp as possible, "hustled" in firewood for the night, and cooked supper. It continued raining and sleeting. All in all, we had a rough sort of a day. The night was divided into watches, so that a fire could be kept up for Colgate.

Saturday, November 4th.—We decided to leave our antlers and all other unnecessary things with Jerry, and lighten our loads as much as possible. Spencer walked up to get him to come down with horses and "pack" the things to his cabin. Keeley, Abe, and I went down to get the raft off the rocks, John remaining in camp to take care of Colgate. After two hours' hard work in the water, we got the raft off and pulled it ashore. Returning to camp, we built a rousing big fire and soon dried all our stuff. Spencer returned at three o'clock and said that Jerry would be down in the morning. We got in firewood for the night. It rained hard nearly all day. Colgate is not as well today as he was yesterday; I am afraid it is due to the wetting he got.

Sunday, November 5th. — We got up at daylight and packed up all the things we intended taking with us. Placing them on Spencer's raft, we carefully let it down the rapid to where the other lay, and transferred one-half the load to our raft. Jerry came down about ten o'clock to get the things we intended leaving with him. Having helped him pack the horses, we said good-by to him again and started down the river at eleven o'clock, with Keeley and Spencer in the lead. Several pretty bad rapids were passed, and the first island was sighted about half-past eleven. Finding the right-hand channel too shallow, we were obliged to take the left-hand, which has some rather bad rocks at the end of the island. Spencer and Keeley stuck, but got off without much difficulty. By keeping more to the left, we got through without trouble, and all made a landing below the island, on the right bank. Abe went down the river to examine the rapids below. This island is merely a gravel bar, with a few pine trees on it. I have no doubt that in summer the right-hand channel is practically dry. A large creek comes into the river just below the island; it drains a fine flat, that I examined some days before and found full of elk and bear signs. Abe returned, and having found a landing-place below, we started again at about half-past one P.M. and made a good run until we came to a worse rapid than any we had yet seen. Spencer and Keeley tried to keep along the right-hand bank and stuck fast on a rock; they motioned us to keep to the center. This brought us into the worst of the water, with large boulders on every side. We were going along at a tremendous rate, when two large rocks loomed up on each side of us, the water falling vertically several feet below them. Thinking it out of the question to pass them, and fully expecting an upset, I shouted to Colgate to hold fast to the posts. We were so fortunate, however, as to get exactly between them, and our raft shot over the drop into the quieter water below. Keeley afterward remarked: "I thought you fellows were goners that time, sure! We couldn't see anything of you after you took the jump." Making a landing below, we went up to help Spencer and Keeley; but they had jumped into the water above their waists and lifted the raft off the rock, and were leading it down along the shore.

Making another examination of the river, we found several stiff rapids—one in particular, where the river narrowed down and went through a gorge. The waves were over four feet high, but the rocks were all hidden by high water. Our raft went ahead, and we had no trouble until we came to the gorge. Here we rolled around like an ocean steamer and came very near upsetting. It's lucky the rocks were covered. The waves struck Abe, who stood in the bow, above the waist, and came near carrying him off the raft. A landing was made, to wait for the other raft, which, however, passed us and took the lead. We found no more bad places; and after going perhaps three-quarters of a mile, we saw that Spencer and Keeley had landed and were motioning us toward them. Although we worked as hard as we could, we could not quite reach the bank, and came near getting caught on some large rocks at the mouth of a creek which comes in from the right. As we passed the other raft we threw out a rope, which fell short. Spencer, however, caught a second rope, and was dragged off his feet into the water. He held on and snubbed the raft, so that we managed to land about twenty yards below them. It being about half-past three P.M., we decided to camp. It has rained hard all day, and every one is wet. Our camp is on a damp flat, with very little dry wood. Some put up the tent and fly, others cut and carried in wood until after dark. After supper, we laid a raised floor of dry cedar under the fly, to put our provisions on, and made a big fire, to dry our blankets. We did not get to bed until after two o'clock A.M. The dogs have been excitedly sniffing the air, and, from the signs we have seen, elk must frequent the flat.

79

Monday, November 6th.—We got up at daylight, and after breakfast Abe and I walked down the river three miles. The walking is harder than the rafting. On the way down we saw old camps and choppings of surveyors. It has rained hard all night, and the river is very high today. We saw two very bad rapids, besides many minor ones. Got back to camp at twelve o'clock and found that Spencer and Keeley had made a bow oar, as the water is getting too deep in places to use poles advantageously. Started down the river, with Spencer and Keeley in the lead. We all had exceptionally good luck in missing big boulders a dozen times or more. Spencer made a landing on the second island and helped us land by the aid of a rope (our raft is heavier and harder to manage than theirs). The left-hand channel was found to be too dangerous to run, as the current makes directly against a ledge of sharp rocks, which we could not pass. The right-hand channel is still more dangerous, for the current sweeps against a large rock in the centre of the river. On the right side of it there are some six large boulders, reaching to the shore. To get by this point safely, it would have been necessary to run the rafts between the big rock and the island, which was obviously impossible in the swift current. We therefore landed on the island, and let the rafts, by ropes, down past the big rock to the foot of the island. This prevented us from examining the river beyond. We could see the waves of a very long and hard rapid below us. There was, however, no alternative but to run ahead and take the chances of finding a fall below. Spencer and Keeley went ahead. We climbed a big pile of driftwood, which the water in freshet time had piled up twenty feet high, and watched them. We saw them enter the rapid, then make a swift shoot out of sight to the right. Their disappearance was so sudden that it almost took our breath away. After a minute's anxious watching, we saw them below the rapid, mere specks in the distance, and found out afterward that they had several "close shaves." We entered the rapid in the centre. The waves were the highest we had yet seen, and we would have been upset if we had not been careful in balancing the raft. These rapids are two hundred yards long, and although the roughest water we had experienced so far, there were no rocks in sight. The river banks are perpendicular at this point, and we could not have landed if we had wished to. Below the rapid is a very deep pool over half a mile long. We found Spencer and Keeley landed on a nice, dry island covered with trees, and as it was half-past three, camp was made. On the island we found the only fresh signs of man (Indians) we had yet seen. There is a trail crossing the river at this point. Evidently the Indians camp here in summer when crossing from the Lo-Lo to the trail on the divide to the south.

We have been out four days now, and have not made much more than ten miles. Keeley is anxious to "turn the rafts loose" and trust to luck in running through, but the others do not consider it safe at all, as we don't know what is below us. It continues to rain hard, and we are pretty well tired out. Our things are all so wet that we have decided to remain here tomorrow. Some of us will dry the blankets, clothes, and provisions, and the rest will go down the river some distance to examine the rapids. A comfortable camp was made and a rousing big fire built. I tried fishing, but had no success, owing to high water. This island is one hundred yards long by twenty-five wide. We found some old tepee-poles and a sweat-bath. The right-hand channel is easy to ford in low water.

Tuesday, November 7th—It was clear this morning, and we were up and through breakfast soon after daylight. Abe decided to go down the river and examine the rapids. We had much trouble in landing him, being obliged to tie the raft with a long rope, and pole and row hard for the shore. The rest of us busied ourselves around camp—some dried blankets, others provisions; Spencer made a bow oar for us. Abe did not get in until dark, very tired and hungry, having had no food but a small piece of bread since morning. He had walked eight miles down the river, and reported the first five miles fair going, but the last three a continuous rapid of very swift water, owing to the exceptional fall of the river-bed. He thinks we cannot run these rapids at all, and will have to let the rafts down by ropes all the way.

Wednesday, November 8th.—We made an exceptionally early start this morning, and made five miles in a very short time, with three stops. The runs were exciting, but not dangerous. On the way down Abe called my attention to a pile of rocks on a high bluff, which he had observed the preceding day and named "Monk's Point," owing to their wonderful likeness to the figure of a hooded monk seated on a rock, with his head bent down, as in thought. We landed at two large eddies, from which we could see the river below take a sudden shoot down, like a mill-race. We passed a beautiful creek, which empties into the river from the left in a succession of miniature falls. John went with Keeley and Spencer today.

Four of us went down to examine Abe's bad rapids, and John stayed with the rafts. We found by far the worst rapids we had yet seen. The current was extremely swift for a mile, and the river full of boulders. Then the river narrowed, and in the centre was a very large rock, which left narrow channels on each side, and these were full of rocks. Below it was still worse—more boulders and worse water. It was clear that we would upset a good many times before getting through this rapid if we were to try to run it; and should we fail to make a landing, we would be carried into a row of rocks that would smash us up completely. We cannot lower the rafts by ropes from the right-hand shore, owing to perpendicular banks in many places. It would be unsafe to leave Colgate on the raft while passing through the worst places, and the right-hand bank is so steep and rough that he cannot be helped along it at all. We returned toward evening and made camp. Tried fishing, but got only one strike. Some of us think we are at the canyon, but Spencer thinks not.

Thursday, November 9th — We awoke to find it drizzling and cold this morning. Got ready as soon as possible and started to cross the river. About two hundred yards below the camp there is a fall in the river; and to be sure that we would not be caught in the current (from which escape would be impossible, and which would carry us over the falls), we pulled our rafts upstream to the head of the eddies and started across from there. Spencer and Keeley took the lead, and made the gravel bar just at the head of the rapid. The left-hand channel was all right, and after running aground on some small rocks, they made the opposite shore and landed. We in turn made the bar, but owing to bad poling our raft turned sidewise in the channel. I jumped out into shallow water, and with a rope tried to hold the stern upstream, but was promptly swept off my feet, and was wet to the neck before I could regain them. We landed some yards below the other raft. Here we all got off, except Colgate, who could not walk along the rocky shore, and Keeley who was to guide the raft with a pole around the rocks. The rest of us let it down the shore with a long rope. Things went smoothly enough until we got to the large rock in the centre of the stream. The water was so terrific that we thought it best to take Colgate off the raft while passing this place. We helped Colgate up to a small flat just back of the river, and John stayed to assist him. Then two of us took the end of the rope down the river, and one stood just above the rock to snub the raft when it entered the narrow channel. The raft was allowed to run downstream through the worst water, about thirty yards. We then tried to snub it, but its momentum was too much for us, and we were all dragged along through the water and over the rocks for some yards. The next mile was very hard work. We had little space to work in, and were pulled off our feet and dragged a good many times. When about fifty yards from the small eddy which we had picked out as our camping place, we attempted to run the raft between some large rocks. It moved so fast, however, that we could not stop it, and it ran aground on a large gravel bar or point. It was raining hard, and Colgate was so cold that we thought it best to build a fire for him immediately.

Keeley would not let his raft down with the rope, but insisted on running the rapids. We didn't think it the best plan, but as it was his raft, we said no more about it. Keeley, Spencer, and Abe went back. The last named was to stand at a point where the current made into the shore and throw them a rope in case they failed to land; then they would lead down from there, and thus escape the worst water. John and I unloaded our raft, got in wood for the night, and tried to get a fire going for Colgate. Everything was soaked, and it took us over an hour to get the fire started. Colgate is so stiff that he cannot move. Just before dark Abe came to camp and told us that Keeley had failed to land, and that their raft had upset on a large rock; that they were in a bad position, and as nearly all our provisions are on their raft, we must try to get it off tonight. We gathered all the ropes we could find and hurried up to where they were. The raft was sidewise on the rocks, and about half of it was held under the water by the current. Spencer had a narrow escape from drowning, being nearly washed away when the raft went under. Although we worked hard, we could not budge the raft; so we put a rope to the bow and another to the stern, and fastened them to trees. I built a fire with a piece of dry cedar, while Abe helped Spencer and Keeley to get ashore on the rope. It was now quite dark and we had a rough time walking back to camp. After supper a large fire was built. Spencer has a great knack of making a good fire out of almost anything. We put up our tent and dried our few blankets as best we could. Half our bedding is on the other raft. We had a very hard day, and everyone is completely tired out. It does not rain now and is growing very cold.

Friday, November 10th—Although fairly tired out last night, we found it difficult to sleep because of the cold. There being insufficient covering and our clothes thoroughly drenched, it is not surprising that we were up and through a hasty breakfast soon after daylight. Upon looking at our raft; just above camp, we found quite a lot of ice on it. It is cold and clear. Immediately after breakfast we went up to the other raft and found it as firmly lodged as it was the night before. The water seems to have fallen slightly. We hastily constructed a small raft of three logs, held together by ropes. Keeley went on this to the raft in the river. The raft was pulled back, and Spencer went over in the same manner. The canvas covering of the load was loosened, and the provisions were loaded on the small raft and safely landed; the rest of the cargo in like manner. The load being off, we found it possible to dislodge the raft from the rocks, and we pulled it into shore a few yards below. Keeley and Spencer were stiff with cold, so we built a fire and warmed up before proceeding farther.

We decided that it was safer to carry the provisions overland on our backs than to trust them to the raft. Some of us did this while the others let the raft down by ropes, arriving at camp at half past three, tired and hungry. After dinner, having a little daylight left, some got in the night's firewood, while the others made a hasty examination of the river below us for a quarter of a mile. Upon their return they reported the water tremendously swift and that the rocks were more numerous and dangerous than any we had yet seen; in fact, they saw one place ahead that looked impassable, but did not have time to get down near it. This is very disagreeable news, for our ropes are becoming frayed and weak from constant contact with sharp rocks, and will not endure much more work of this kind. In case they should break when we are letting a raft through a bad place, it would mean the probable death of those on board, and the certain loss of the provisions. We are also worried about Colgate, who seems to be failing very rapidly in strength and in mind. He hardly says a word all day except when he is spoken to, or at meal-time, when he is given his food. He sits and gazes for hours with a vacant stare at the river or the rocks. His legs look very bad indeed, and are evidently mortified from the knees down. We found today that our flour was getting very low; only about forty pounds are left. We decided to eat no more of it at present, but to live on cornmeal and beans as long as they last. We are out of fresh meat. I tried to catch some fish, but they would not rise. We hope this may be the much-talked-of canyon and that we will soon be through it.

Saturday, November 11th— It is still cold and clear. We went down the river a long way this morning, and were horrified to find that we were absolutely "stuck." Half a mile below camp is a ledge of rocks, and a rapid through which we cannot take a raft. Below this are two more places still worse. Every one gave his opinion of his own accord, that we could not get our rafts farther down the river. Our position is as follows: We have barely one week's short allowance of flour left. All our other provisions, except a few pounds of cornmeal and beans, and a handful of salt each, are exhausted. The shores of the river are a mass of irregular rocks. Numerous hedges or cliffs, some of them hundreds of feet high, rise vertically above the river and project into it. The mill-sides adjacent are steep and rocky, and covered with dense brush. Many of the ledges are so precipitous that it is all an able-bodied man can do to hang to bushes and climb around them on narrow clefts or steps in the rock. Most of us are considerably weakened from exposure, and are not in a fit condition to walk. Owing to the character of the country and our enfeebled condition, we cannot hope to accomplish more than four or five miles a day on foot. As nearly as we can estimate, we are fifty or fifty-five miles from civilization (Wilson's ranch, twenty miles below the forks). We know nothing whatever of the river ahead of us, of the obstructions we will meet with, or even if we can get through at all by this route. The dreaded Black Canyon is yet before us. Worst of all is the fact that Colgate cannot possibly walk, and it is absolutely impossible to help or carry him around the bad places along the river. His condition grows worse hourly. His legs are in a frightful condition, and the odor that comes from them is almost unendurable. He is perceptibly weaker than he was yesterday, and his mind is so far gone that he has lately appreciated no efforts that have been made to make him comfortable. On our return to camp, at half-past two PM, we drew to one side and discussed every plan that could be thought of—not a stone was left unturned. If we stay with him, we can do nothing but ease his last moments and bury him, because it is impossible for him ever to get well again. His sickness is, besides, of such a character that he may linger in a stubborn semi-conscious condition for several days, during which a large portion of our remaining provisions will be consumed. We cannot even take him back and leave him with Jerry Johnson, while some of us go out on snowshoes for assistance. With no sign of game in the neighborhood, and the river full of floating ice so that the fish will not rise, were we to leave half our provisions here and one man to care for Colgate, he would probably starve before succor could reach him, while such a drain on the meagre supplies would render the chances considerably less of the others ever reaching civilization. We all feel that it is clearly a case of trying to save five lives, or sacrificing them in order to perform the last sad rites for poor Colgate. To remain longer with Colgate is to jeopardize to the very doors of folly all our lives—not in the cause of humanity, for Colgate is beyond any appreciation of such kindness—but for sentiment solely. We have exhausted every resource, and feel that we have gone to the extreme limit of duty toward Colgate in our endeavors to get him back to civilization. Our own families and friends have now a just claim upon us, and we must save ourselves if possible. We therefore have decided to strike down the river, and, with good luck, some us may get through, unless we encounter a bad snow-storm. Every one feels very much dispirited having to leave Colgate. There was hardly a word spoken by any one tonight.

Sunday, November 12th—This morning we made up our packs, taking nothing but provisions, two flat stew-pans that fitted inside one another, the smaller being filled with coffee, and two small frying-pans. Abe will take his camera, which is very light. I cut a roll of exposures out of mine and threw the box away. When we came to cross the river, we found it was not so easy as it looked. We had to reach a small point of rocks, fifty yards below us, on the opposite side of the river. If we failed in this (and the current was against us, as it made in to our side of the river), we would be carried down into the big ledge, and that would be the end of us. Some were in favor of trusting to luck in trying to cross. If we got across, all right; if we didn't, all right too! Others proposed going down on our side of the river, but this was objected to on the ground that this side is likely not to be so open as the south hillside, and would have more snow; besides we would have to cross at the forks anyway, and while we had our rafts we had better cross here. Abe suggested that we fell a very large white pine tree, which stands on the bank and seems to lean toward the river, and by fastening a long rope to the end we could drift half-way across and then pull ashore with our sweeps, while the rope held us from going down the stream. The tree is about forty-four inches in diameter. Keeley began the cutting. Others worked at various things, and I went hunting, in the hope of getting some fresh meat. I saw no fresh signs of game at all except one grouse. On my return I tried fishing, with no better success. Our food for two days had been cornmeal and beans. It slowed a little today, and is cloudy and cold. We start on our tramp tomorrow, taking nothing but provisions, guns, and the clothes on our backs. Colgate is very badly off tonight. He has great difficulty in breathing. It would not surprise me at all to see him collapse at any moment. I told him today that we could raft no farther and would have to walk, but it seemed to make no impression whatever upon him.

Monday, November 13th. —Daylight found us up and through breakfast, and we were delighted to find it perfectly clear and cool. It took us until one o'clock to fell the big tree, as we had to fall another large tree against it and hitch ropes to its branches, so that it would fall into the river. When it did fall it fairly shook the earth, and, to our disappointment, the top sank fifteen feet under the water. Still, the branches that were available reached nearly half-way across the river. Abe and Keeley tied one end of the long rope firmly to the limbs as far as they could reach, and the other end was fastened to the raft. We determined to test the strength of the rope and to land Abe on the opposite bank if possible, so that when we crossed with the big load we could throw him a rope, and he could help us land. Abe,

Keeley, and I pushed off and got half-way across without the slightest trouble, but had to pull for dear life to get across the current. Landing Abe, we returned for the rest and made the trip safely, although we had a close call to an upset on account of the swift current, which nearly sucked one side of the raft down. After landing, we cut the raft loose, to see where the current would take it; it was whirled downstream for two hundred yards and jammed to a mass of big rocks to the left of the middle of the river.

Poor Colgate was so far gone that he could not remember his family, nor did he make any remarks or request concerning them. We made him as comfortable as we could, left him what necessaries we thought he might require in the brief period he had yet to live, and, shouldering our packs, we started sadly down the river. Although Colgate's head was turned toward us, he made no motion or outcry as he saw us disappear, one by one, around the bend.

We walked over some very rough country until we came to a small creek about two miles down, which we crossed on a log. Our path then led through a rather open flat, and we made camp on a small sand-bar at about four o'clock, having walked two and one-half miles. A small, slanting shelter of pine boughs was made, under which we lay down to sleep.

Tuesday, November 14th. —We had a fairly comfortable camp last night and got several hours' sleep, which was doing well, considering the cold and lack of all covering. After a breakfast of coffee and a small allowance of bread, we resumed our walks down the river at eight o'clock. We shifted and changed our packs a good deal today, as they begin to grow heavy and cut our shoulders. Besides our packs, Keeley carried an axe, and Abe, John, and I had a gun apiece. The first part of the day our route was through a fine flat. We think it is the flat below Bald Mountain, in which they say there is a warm spring. On a small side-hill we found a trail, which led back into the mountains, and by the side of the trail some fairly fresh signs of Indian choppings and "blazes." Some of us were anxious to stop for a day and get an elk, the fresh signs being numerous, but the majority favored going ahead; so we kept on. After leaving the flat, the country began to grow rougher and the side-hills became steep, slippery, rocky, and brushy—all at once, as it were. On one of these side-hills we found an old line chopped out by a surveying party. The walking was very difficult, and we had to use both our hands and feet in climbing. We have kept an eye on the river, and are satisfied that we were very sensible in abandoning the rafts. We have seen a good many places where we could not possibly have taken a raft through. We passed a fall of some six feet, about half-past one o'clock, which had bad rocks above and below it. The river is beautiful: I have never seen such clear-looking water. We walked until three o'clock, having made, we think, five miles. Abe killed a grouse today, and I caught two fish weighing half a pound each. We enjoyed them hugely for supper, making broth from the grouse and frying the fish. Our camp is good, and we are fairly comfortable.

Wednesday, November 15th. —We made a breakfast of tea and a little bread, and started down the river at 8 o'clock. The character of the country was somewhat the same as yesterday—small flats and very difficult side-hills. About noon we passed a fine large creek, which runs through a deep gorge and flows into the river from the south. The lack of nourishing food, loss of sleep, and exposure is beginning to tell on us all; we are very weak and unsteady on our feet. Everything that will lighten our load has been thrown away. During the day we killed three grouse. Abe and John both had watches, but John's stopped after getting it wet in the river a week ago. For safety, Abe had been carrying his watch in his hip-pocket. Today he slipped and fell down on a rock, smashing the watch. The crystal was pulverized so that it resembled salt. Our last and only timepiece is thus ruined.

We were caught at dark in a miserable flat some distance from the river, making it difficult to obtain water. It began to rain at dark, and continued to rain, sleet, and snow all night. We had trouble to secure firewood, and there is not a tree in the vicinity big enough to shelter anyone from the rain, so we got soaking wet and cold, and had no sleep all night. The three grouse were stewed for supper and the bones given to the dogs, which had eaten hardly a mouthful since November 13th. They are about as weak as we are. Daisy, the black dog, seems to be in the poorest condition. I feel that our chances are rather slim of getting out of the mountains. Every one is tired out and miserable.

Thursday, November 16th. — We got up at daylight and partook of our usual slim breakfast of bread and coffee. The country was very rough today. The first part of our route was over broken, rocky shores. We found more perpendicular bluffs than usual, which we had to climb around. In our weak condition, we found it very hard work to climb up the steep hill-sides. Our guns are a regular nuisance, for we need both hands in climbing. At half past ten we sighted the worst looking bluff we had yet seen, and, upon coming to it, found our way blocked by a large and very rapid creek.

We stopped here and made a little coffee for lunch. Being unable to find any tree on which to cross the creek, we were obliged to cut one down. Owing to the rain and sleet blowing down the river, the upper side of our tree was icy and slippery. Had any one fallen off, he would have been swept down into the river and drowned. The water is so rapid that it is milky white, from rushing over and between the rocks. Once across, we had a hazardous climb of an almost perpendicular side-hill for about one thousand feet. It was very slippery and icy, and we were all tired out on reaching the top. It is very lucky that no one fell. Following the ridge for a quarter of a mile, we made a descent to the river again, when, on turning a small point, we came upon the Black Canyon. There was no mistaking it this time! I do not think any view in the mountains ever impressed me as this one did. Not even the magnificent view from the top of the Twisp River divide at the head of Lake Chelan, where the whole Cascade Range of mountains, with its wonderfully varied scenery, can be seen in every direction from seventy-five to one hundred and twenty-five miles. The view did not impress me so much with its grandeur as with an indefinable dread weirdness. It immediately associated itself in my mind with death. The surroundings seemed, for some reason, indescribably well suited to the thought—probably owing to the weakened state of my body and mind. The river before us for several hundred yards was a broad, deep, still pool, which reflected perfectly the steep rocky bank opposite and the muggy sky above. The river gradually narrowed down as it approached the succession of mighty rock walls, which were so close together that they seemed to meet at the top. A hazy curtain seemed to hang before the tremendous gap, and behind this all seemed black. We could hear the sullen booming of the rapids in the distance, which had a peculiarly unpleasant sound, probably owing to their being enclosed in the huge rocky walls. I should judge that the highest point that we can see from here is at least three thousand feet above the river. I think we all realize now that we have a difficult task ahead. We are very weak, and if Spencer is right in his belief that the canyon is eight or ten miles long, it will take at least two and a half or three days of hard climbing to get through it, if indeed it is passable at all. We were so tired that it was decided that Abe, Spencer, and John should go down the river a short distance and select a suitable camp, while Keeley and I tried the fishing. Never had I seen a finer hole for trout; and in the clear water we could see fish of all sizes lying quietly here and there or swimming lazily about. We had no spoons and no large hooks. We had tied several small flies together, and put a lead weight two feet in front of them to enable us to cast out; then we drew them slowly toward us. We hooked plenty of fish, but they were so large that they broke our hooks time after time. I am certain that one I had almost on shore, when he broke my hook, weighed at least five pounds—it was a Dolly Varden or bull trout—while Keeley lost one that was considerably larger. After fishing for two hours and losing thirty or more fish and about twenty hooks, we gave up in despair, and returned to camp with one half-pound trout, which Keeley had landed. The others looked so disappointed when we returned to camp with only one small fish that we went out again and managed to catch two more, of nearly one pound apiece. These, added to the grouse Abe had shot, made us a first-rate supper. We stewed the fish, drinking the broth, which was excellent, and divided the flesh evenly in our drinking-cups. If we only had one good, strong trollingspoon, we could catch fifty pounds of fish easily. Our camp is dismally cold and wet, but luckily we have plenty of wood near at hand. We made a big fire for the night. We saw that our best chance for food was fish, and after supper we hunted for something from which to make a spoon. Spencer produced a piece of copper wire, which he used to clean his pipe. Keeley made one spoon from the bowl of a teaspoon, while I made another by hammering out a silver half-dollar. Money is some good in the mountains after all. When finished they looked very well, and will undoubtedly attract the fish; but we still have to rely on the small hooks to hold them. Upon counting the hooks, I find that we have twenty-four left.

Friday, November 17th—We started at eight o'clock this morning, determined to do our best toward getting through the canyon. Our route led along a very steep, brushy hill-side. We found an old game trail, which led slanting up the side-hill. We followed this until we were at an elevation of perhaps fifteen hundred feet above the river, when the trail was lost. I guess the game does not pass through the canyon, but strikes back from the river into the hills. We had to be very careful of our footing, as the hillside is so steep that we would probably land in the river, or at any rate over some of the numerous precipices, if we were to slip. The south side of the canyon is vertical at this point, and we believe that this side is so also at the river; it was almost vertical where we passed along today. We feel that we were very lucky to have crossed on the raft, for the walls opposite us are impassable. We found more snow today than we had yet seen, probably owing to the short time the sun shines in the canyon. We continued walking with great care all day, and made a difficult descent to the river in order to camp on a small point, where we could get wood and water. Although we worked very hard, we have not accomplished more than two and one-half or three miles. Abe shot a blue grouse today. We made camp on the point, and built a shelter to keep out the cold wind that sweeps down the canyon. It is necessary that we should sleep all we possibly can, to keep up our strength. The black dog looked so miserable tonight that I thought it the kindest act all around to kill her. This I did by shooting her in the head with Spencer's revolver. We then hung her up and skimmed her, and when the flesh got cold we cut off the best portions and made a strong broth—strong in every sense of the word. Into the broth we put a tablespoonful of flour. The soup was good, but the flesh was tough and strong. Although nearly starved, only one of the three remaining dogs would touch the meat. By our camp is a very large, hollow cedar tree, the base spreading out over six feet. We made a fire in the hollow base. There was a strong draught, so we soon had a regular furnace going. The flames shot out of the top for some distance, and the heat finally became so great that we were obliged to leave our shelter and stretch out on the rocks. We found a portion of last summer's *Spokane Review* and a cleaning-rod for a 45-calibre rifle on the spot where we made our shelter. Evidently some one was up the river this far last summer. We feel somewhat encouraged by these signs of man. Abe took several photographs today of the canyon walls and the "crowd." We tried fishing, but had no strikes.

Saturday, November 18th—We started out by climbing up the side of the canyon, taking every available chance to get forward. The walking is harder than any we have yet had. Many times we were stopped by high perpendicular faces of rock. We had to go up or down for considerable distances to get around some of these; others we had to cross, and trust to luck not to fall. Keeley is particularly good at finding all available foot-holds and paths. He has been a splendid fellow all through, doing all he could, and not grumbling at all. Expecting to cut around some bad places, we climbed straight up for a long distance, but found nothing better. We got into moose-brush covered with snow, and our feet slipped from under us at every few steps. Nothing seems to do us so much harm in our weak condition as the jarring resulting from a fall. After we got out of the moose-brush we ran into a thicket, and then climbed a snowy side-hill through brush and down timber. Looking back from the top of this ridge, we saw Bald Mountain about fifteen miles to the northeast. At three o'clock we struck what looked like a trail, but it led us to a point where there was a perpendicular descent of several hundred feet; it was evidently not a trail at all. The view from here is extended and grand, but we are not in a condition to admire scenery. We were utterly tired out, and proposed camping. Spencer tried to get to the river, but came back and reported that he could not get down; so we decided to camp about fifty yards farther down, in a bunch of rocks and near a little creek. It took me nearly one hour to work my way down to the creek and bring back a pail of water, but we found a much easier path later. We had difficulty in finding firewood for the night. A few boughs were cut to lie upon, but I fear no one will be able to sleep. We can easily see the rocky bluff just above last night's camp. We have made less than one and one-half miles down the river today. Every one is growing weaker, and the flour is getting very low. Abe killed one grouse today, and tonight some one sang, "We'll be angels by and by," and no one seemed to disagree with the singer.

Sunday, November 19th—John decided to abandon his gun, so he left it hanging to a tree in camp. We felt that we must work hard today, which we did. Time walking improved, and we found occasional old game trails. We lost much valuable time, however, by following one which took us up into the hills. We passed many bad places, and it is a wonder to me that no one slips and falls, all being so weak. Two of us have no hobnails left in our boots, and three of us are very footsore. We feel encouraged by having seen that we are a good way below Bald Mountain, and we ought not to be more than fifteen miles from the forks of the river, where there is a trail leading down to Wilson's ranch. Fresh deer signs were seen today. At four o'clock we reached the end of the canyon, and camped near a small sand-bar. We built two large parallel fires, but did not succeed in keeping warm. We have only enough flour left for one more meal. Not being able to sleep, from weakness and cold, I sat thinking of what our friends were doing in the outside world, when my attention was attracted by the two little dogs, Montana and Idaho. Poor little Montana very far gone, and so weak and thin that it is a surprise to me that she can keep up with us. All the hair is worn from her legs by the sharp rocks. Tonight she lay down as close as she could to the fire and extended her four legs, to keep them warm; still she shivered, I suppose from weakness. Idaho, her mate, is much stronger, and seemed to realize Montana's condition, for she came and lay partly on top of her and partly on the outside of her, so as to protect the side exposed to the cold. I do not recall ever having heard of a similar case of animal sympathy.

Monday, November 20th. — For breakfast we ate the last of the bread. We worked for all that was in us today, and were favored with pretty good walking in comparison to what we have been having. We were able to keep near the river a good part of the time, instead of having to continually climb around vertical walls. We staggered a good deal today from weakness, and Abe, who has stood it splendidly so far, is also beginning to break down, principally from lack of sleep, having averaged only about one hour a night for seven nights. We found a few frozen haw-berries along our route, which we ate. Our violent cravings of hunger have left us somewhat, and our stomachs seem to have accustomed themselves to do with very little. Fully six miles were covered today, and camp was made during a cold rain in a damp flat. Abe went to look for deer for half an hour, but saw none, although fresh signs were plentiful in the snow. Keeley caught a fish weighing one pound, of which we made broth, and had that and coffee for supper. It was very difficult to get enough wood to last all night.

Tuesday, November 21st. —We had a little piece of bacon, weighing about one-eighth of a pound, which we used to grease the pan with in baking bread. The flour being exhausted, we made a broth of that this morning. Abe went for deer, but got none, as it began to snow. Most of us are too weak to walk without breakfast, and can barely stagger around. Keeley caught three fish which we ate, and started down the river at eleven o'clock, walking very slowly and often stumbling and falling down. After going about a mile we found a nice fishing-hole. Keeley caught four and I two, making six fine fish in all—a veritable feast. I had no control over my arms. When I whirled the spoon around to throw it into the river, it was just as likely to fly back of or above me. We soon made camp and stewed the fish. The dogs got quite a meal of fish bones, and seemed to feel relieved.

Wednesday, November 22d. —It snowed about two inches during the night, and this morning it was dark and squally. We tried hard to catch fish, but did not get a strike. One small fish kept following Keeley's spoon to the shore, but would not strike. Getting desperate, he shot at it with his revolver, but missed it. Seeing it was no use to fish, we made some tea and started slowly down the river. The majority decided that we would walk no farther after today, but would try to build a rude raft if we could find light driftwood that required no cutting from which to build it. Our feet felt as heavy as lead, and falls were frequent. We notice that the hills are getting very low now. Abe, who has been keeping account of our daily progress, estimated that we were about nine or ten miles from the forks this morning. The rapids are no longer dangerous, and most of us feel that, if we made a raft, we could make Wilson's ranch in a day or two at the most. If we could kill no grouse or trout, we could eat one of the dogs to keep up our strength. The walking was rather hard, as we had to leave the river bank to climb around vertical walls of rock several times. We had made, perhaps, one mile when we struck a particularly bad place. I got too high up to cross easily and thus dropped behind the others some distance, but found Abe waiting for me when I got down. I was tempted to throw away my gun, but disliked very much to part with it, as it is my favorite. We continued slowly down along the side-hill, and seeing some hawberries on the river bank, went down to eat them. I said: "Abe, it seems to me that our friends must know of our position, and that they would try to get up this river as far as they could toward us. They certainly know that this is the route we are mostly likely to take, and that we must be working down this way!" Abe said in reply, "I have thought it all over and believe they will send some one; but I allow them three or four days yet." On turning the next point, we saw two men hurrying toward us. Thinking they were of our party I said, "I wonder what's the matter? Perhaps they have seen a deer and want us to shoot it!" but he replied, "I am afraid some one has fallen into the river." As they approached nearer, we saw they were not of our party, and a moment later, Abe recognized our old-time shooting chum, Sergt. Guy Norton, of the Fourth Cavalry. With him was Lieut. Charles P. Elliott. It expresses it mildly to say we were overjoyed to see them. Our tired limbs seemed filled with new life, and we followed them briskly to their first boat, about two hundred yards below. Abe, who was very much interested in his estimate of distances, asked Mr. Elliott how far it was to the "forks," and learned, with much satisfaction, that the confluence of the south fork with the Kooskooskee was about seven miles distant. When we arrived where Mr. Elliott's boat was lying, we found the rest of our party and two soldiers—Sergt. Smart and Private Norlin, of Mr. Elliott's company—and three civilian boatmen, Messrs. Lamonthe, Burke, and Winn. They had a fire started and oatmeal and bacon cooking when we arrived. Mr. Elliott advised us to eat moderately at first, until we gradually accustomed ourselves again to food. While enjoying our first meal, we learned all the details of the meeting of the two parties. Mr. Elliott's party was making its way up the river with two boat-loads of provisions. So swift and rough was the water that a portage was necessary at nearly every rapid. They had gotten the smaller boat over the last rapid below; and while the balance of the party returned for the other boat, Mr. Elliott and Roary Burke sat down on a rock near the first boat and waited for them. While thus seated, their attention was attracted by the barking of Winn's dog, and when they looked around Burke saw one of our little white terriers through an opening under the rocks. Not knowing what it was, Mr. Elliott asked for a gun, but soon discovered that what he saw was a small white dog. The terrier "Idaho" soon made her presence known by violent barking. At the same time Spencer, who had, however, seen the two men first, appeared above the rocks, followed closely by John and Keeley.

Mr. Elliott, seeing Spencer, accosted him with: "Hello! Who in God's name are you?"

Spencer replied: "My name is Spencer, the guide of the Carlin party. Who are you?

After informing Spencer that a rescuing party was at hand, Mr. Elliott asked, "How is everybody?" to which Spencer replied, "All well, but hungry as h—l!"

A bear that is stopped or turned by pepper spray will be affected for about 10 minutes, more or less, depending on many factors. Once a bear is turned get to safety immediately—out of the area, to a vehicle or dwelling, or even up a tree if that's the only escape available. Just because a bear is stopped for the moment doesn't mean it won't come back soon. (August 93, p.50)

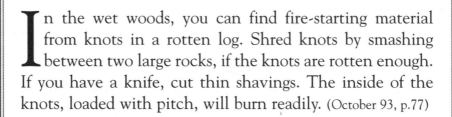

In the wet woods, you can find fire-starting material from knots in a rotten log. Shred knots by smashing between two large rocks, if the knots are rotten enough. If you have a knife, cut thin shavings. The inside of the knots, loaded with pitch, will burn readily. (October 93, p.77)

Fruit, sweet drinks, syrups—even meat—all draw in bad bugs. When picnicking or camping, keep foodstuffs covered and dispose of trash promptly. Minimize your fleshy target area by wearing long pants, shoes and high socks. Bug repellents don't seem to prevent stings from a determined bee or hornet, though tests show that spraying repellent at a swarm will often turn it away.

Handwarmers that outdoorsmen use during cold weather can actually cause hands to get colder. Your hands sweat from the heat that builds up when they're kept in pockets or inside mittens. The resulting moisture on your hands—or even in the fabric of your handwear—can make them become colder than ever when you expose them to the air again. To prevent this, it is wise to keep handwarmers out of your gloves or mittens unless they are made of breathable material such as rag wool. Also, keeping handwarmers in large, ventilated pockets will allow air to circulate and keep things dry and toasty. (December 94, p.52)

One of the most important things you can have with you when you are icefishing on a big lake is a compass. You might think that sounds kind of silly, but a heavy snowstorm, or even a light one with a wind, can erase the shoreline from your view and leave you wondering which direction is north. Even if you have an idea where the shore is, without a compass you may find yourself wandering in a circle instead of moving toward where you want to go. (February 93, p.69)

Drink plenty of fluids when in preparation of a cold day. Hot drinks are best when you're cold, but avoid caffeine—its effects cost you heat. If thirsty, don't eat snow; melt and warm it first if possible.

Camping in snow with comfort. Instead of melting snow, save time and fuel by locating running water. Look along streams for open spots or dig in a low spot of the snow fill streambed. Often, snow banks are high above the surface of the water and there is no convenient way down. Carry a collapsible vinyl bucket and tie 30 feet of alpine cord to the handle. Drop the bucket into the stream and haul up the water. (January 93, p.24)

When snow is unconsolidated, breaking trail can be wearisome. Take shifts and spread the work. The front person breaks for five minutes, then steps aside and lets those behind him pass. He then has easy going at the end. The new first person breaks for five minutes before moving to the end of the line, and so on.

Carry a small whisk broom to brush off boots and gaiters, and a sponge to mop damp spots. Before your trip, remove all food from cardboard packaging and put it in plastic bags. Keep clothing in stuff sacks so they don't accumulate snow while opening and closing your pack.

"More lives are saved by whistles than any other device. They should be standard issue for anyone heading into the backcountry."

—Frank Hubbell, Wilderness Rescue Expert

Building a thermal shelter. Clear snow down to bare ground or ice, and construct a bipod framework. Add more sticks to the side for structural support, and weave in evergreen boughs. If no boughs are available, use parachute or tarp for covering. Put door logs in place and cover structure frame with at least 10 inches of snow. Build a door plug by filling a tarp or rag with snow and tying the end. (January 93, p.99)

One of the cheapest, most efficient fire starters you can take with you camping is a 2-foot-long 2x4. With nothing more than a good pocketknife, you can easily whittle a pile of dry kindling in no time. Stuff this beneath a few twigs and limbs, and the comfort of a warm fire will soon be yours to enjoy. To keep the 2x4 dry, simply store it beneath your vehicles seat or inside a spare tire. (April 93, p.89)

During temperature-gradient metamorphism, when the temperature difference between ground and air is large, bonds between snowflakes are weak. Avalanches are possible on steep slopes holding this type of snow. (December 92, p. 104)

Camping in the snow with comfort. The midnight pit stop. Relieving yourself at night means, at the least, rising from your bag to aim out the tent door. Women have it even harder. A more civil way of handling the business is to carry a one-liter, wide-mouthed Nalgalene bottle, marked with a circle of duct tape so you can feel it in the dark and thus distinguish it from your water bottle. Urinate into the bottle, which with a little bit of practice can be done without getting out of the comfort of your sleeping bag. (January 93, p.24)

Snow Kitchen. Near the tent dig a trench with stairs leading into it. Three feet deep by four feet wide by seven feet long suffices for two people. On one long side make a bench on which you can unroll a foam sleeping pad. On the other make a table. Let the snow kitchen set up for at least a half-hour before using it. This is preferable to cooking in your tent—even if the air temperature is below zero—because steam makes clothing and sleeping bags soggy. (January 93, p.24)

No matter how bad the conditions are, there is always tinder to start a fire in the areas where birch trees grow. One would naturally assume that the dry, dead bark would be better than the green for starting a fire, but this is not true. The best fire starter comes from green bark. Cut into the tree with a knife and pull a section of the bark free. It peels nicely from the trunk. Due to the high sap content in this green bark, it is easily lit and burns exceptionally well.

Large avalanches slide on slopes with an angle averaging between 25 and 55 degrees. The careful traveler will therefore avoid these slopes if factors point to the possibility of avalanches—such as the presence of temperature gradient snow. The safest route to follow is above the potential slide path. Next best is far below the runout zone. If a party has to cross an avalanche path, members should cross one by one. (December 92, p.105)

To obtain dry wood in a frigid or wet environment, find a dead spruce, pine or fir, and cut halfway through the tree, three feet up. Start swaying the tree back and forth, creating a split that will run up the tree. Once down, place the split end on stump, and make another cut halfway through the tree, two feet up. Apply downward pressure, splitting the tree section. Place split sections in a pile until the entire tree has been split. Then use a knife or ax to split tinder and kindling, leaving the larger pieces for fuel. (January 93, p.97)

Used with a little creativity, thickets, overhangs, sage brush and snow moats, which form around trees in winter, can help to break the wind and keep us warmer. The closer to the ground we take shelter, even to the extent of excavating a pit in the snow all the way down to ground level, the warmer we'll be.

Open fractures are extremely dangerous. One of the main risks is infection of the bone itself, which can be crippling or even fatal. In best-case scenarios, all you should do for a broken bone is immobilize it against further damage, using either a splint or a sling, depending on the specific area involved. Then bring trained medical help to the victim or, if necessary, very

carefully bring the victim to a medical professional. (April 22, p57)

Pain, swelling and even numbness may not in themselves mean that a bone is broken. If no fracture is visible (neither open nor angulated), and no crepitus is noticeable to the touch, and if the victim can move the limb freely, most likely the wound does not include a fracture. When in doubt, of course, treat a possible break as a break.

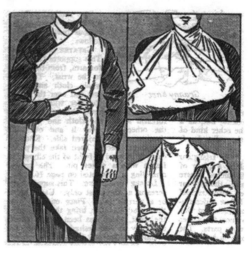

Letting people know your exact route and when you're expected to return will greatly speed any rescue attempts if you're incapacitated and overdue. Don't depend on the memory of a friend or family member. Leave them a written note.

Survival in cold water is a matter of time. In 50° F water, wearing a life jacket and holding still, you have on average 2½ to three hours to live. Without flotation, your time may be cut in half. You must keep afloat by treading water or drown-proofing. Treading water increases the body's cooling rate by 34 percent, drown-proofing by 82 percent.

When whitewater rafting, stay upstream of your boat. If you're downstream, the craft can smash or pin you against an obstruction. If possible, grab the boat's rope from the upstream side and hang onto your paddle with one hand as you float downstream. But if any gear threatens to drag you into danger, let go immediately. (October 93, p.46)

A major part of survival is mental preparation practice. Because when it comes to survival, knowledge must be more than theoretical; you must be able to do what you know. This is where 99 out of 100 outdoorsmen fail. By never making the effort to practice skills (orienteering by compass; building a fire with or without matches; fashioning a shelter; splinting a broken leg) they never own those skills. When an emergency occurs, they must learn on the spot, when the odds are poor. Those who do practice acquire another vital key: confidence. The sense of "I can beat this" pushes aside fear and panic, and furthers one's will to survive.

Of the 8,000 snakebite victims in a given year, only nine to 14 die. The chance of death by snakebite is less than one-half percent. In as many as 20 percent of snakebites no venom is injected into the victim, either because fang penetration was superficial, or because the snake didn't release its full load.

Be alert, or find yourself hurt! When hunting from the same tree stand day after day in blustery fall weather, try using a throw rug or a bit of canvas to cover the platform before you leave. This keeps rain, ice, and snow off the platform; otherwise it could become dangerously slick overnight. Excessive leaning, as when aiming, can tip or dislodge a stand. Be sure you are firmly braced and balanced before pulling the trigger or releasing an arrow. Wear a safety strap. Falling asleep can mean literally that, a sudden fall after you doze off with the warm autumn breeze in your face. Tighten the strap so you only have six to eight inches of slack, and if for some reason you begin to fall, the harness will catch you before you have a chance to tumble off the platform. (November 00, p.92)

WOODS SAFETY. Bring a fluorescent orange vest if there may be other hunters in the woods when you're bird hunting. Wear it when moving between hunting areas or walking into and out of the woods. You can also buy orange bags for safely carrying a turkey out. (October 96, p.95)

Bear trouble? In Alaskan and Canadian trouble zones, carry short-barreled high caliber rifles with open sights; nothing lighter than a 30-06, with a 338 or 375 H&H preferred. Sling these barrel-down so that the gun can be instantly lifted and rolled into shooting position. There is still the need to be calm and steady in the face of terror, and wounding is still a possibility, but the chances for deadly force and accuracy are much better. (Summer 97, p.41)

When you encounter a canine in the woods, or even in a hunting buddy's kennel, don't flash your pearly whites. To a dog, showing teeth means you're ready for a fight, even if you're saying nice doggie in a pleasant, non-threatening voice. Take care to teach young children—as soon as they're old enough—not to grin at pets, strange dogs or even the family pointer or retriever. If a dog approaches, calmly and slowly present only the back of your hand for it to sniff. Otherwise, a sudden snap might take a chunk from your trigger finger. (March 96, p.55)

There are numerous folk remedies for chigger bites. Nail polish is the favorite recommendation; the polish is said to smother the chigger, but there is new information that this is incorrect. Nail polish may still smother the chigger, which we cannot see clinging to the skin's surface. But scratching will remove him too. (May 93, p.50)

Use the strap harness carry when transporting an injured camper. 1. Place strap around victim's waist, crisscrossing it at chest. 2. Elevate victim. Bring strap ends over rescuer's shoulder and down between victim's legs. 3. Bring ends around victim's legs and tie off at rescuer's waist. (August 95, p. 54)

The common mouse and similar members of the *Rodentia* family are often one's best bet for survival food and can be eaten with minimal preparation. Singe away the hair in a flame and place the carcass, guts and all, in the fire's ashes to roast. This is usually far more practical than attempting to build a pit trap for deer, or ranging off on energy-consuming, odds-off, big game hunts; and the mouse, overall, is more completely nutritious than lean venison steak. (April 94, p.52)

Snakes, frogs, young birds, shellfish, insects—all can, in various circumstances, be easily obtained and eaten. But cook them first unless you're at death's door. Eating raw flesh incurs the risk of illness—the last thing anyone needs when weak from hunger. (April 94, p.52)

Everyone who has been exposed to poison ivy once will get it the second time. Some people suffer far more than others, but no one is immune. (August 93, p.80)

Northern Lives

Most of us who run and read do not require proof to know that the way of the musher is hard. The long Alaska winters alone, with none of the accompanying hardships, would ensure that. Probably in no other country on the globe does the prospector and trapper encounter such heart-rending obstacles as in Alaska. A large number of these men whom you meet in that country — those whose lives are spent in the open — are going to get away from it "next fall." They need a larger stake, or they wish to finish just one task; then they intend to hike to the "outside" — as the States is called. But only a small percentage of those rosy dreams ever are realized, for before they know it something has happened that makes their exit from that land less likely than ever before. A bad fall in the glaciers, or a frozen and amputated foot, or hands, nose or ears may have been disfigured from freezing, with the result that they feel that they "belong" very well where they are.

A large number of the men of the Arctic wouldn't live anywhere else. They seem to have been seized with the lure of the Northland — which is there, all right, for those who like it, just as you find men who get fascinated with the desert, and who can't give it up — and once this spell is upon them, you might as well try to induce Mt. Shishaldin to shift positions as attempt to jar them loose from their enthrallment.

We are indebted to A. M. Bailey (an Alaskan of some years' experience) for complete detailed diaries kept by "Sourdoughs" previous to *their respective deaths in different localities of Alaska. In each of these cases they were alone and so far from civilization that, in their terribly weakened condition [could not] reach assistance.*

Note: — This is a correct copy of the diary left by one V. Swanson, known as the "Wildman of Dry Bay," whose body was found on the 18th of August, 1918, by Hardy Trefger and Fred Zastrow, trappers from Dry Bay.

1917

Oct. 28 — Winter has come. Strong wind, two feet of snow.

Nov. 4 — Shot one lynx.

6 — Made one pair of bearskin pants.

8 — Sugar is all gone.

13 — Made two pair of moccasins.

18 — Finished one fur coat of bear, wolf and lynx.

21 — Finished one sleeping bag of bear, goat.

22 — Left eye bothers me. Shot one goat.

26 — Shot one lynx while eating breakfast.

27 — Made one pair of bearpaw snowshoes.

Dec. 1 — Getting bad. Cold for several days, river still open.

4 — River raised six feet in twenty-four hours.

6 — Slush stiffening slowly, making ice.

7 — The wind is so strong that you can't stand upright. Snow getting deeper now.

15 — Very cold and strong wind, impossible to be out without skin clothes.

19 — Snowing, but still very cold. Can't travel. Very little grub; snow too deep and soft for hunting goats. Stomach balking at straight meat, especially lynx.

21 — Shot a goat from the river.

25 — Very cold. A good Christmas dinner. Snow getting hard.

26 — Broke through the ice. Skin clothes saved the day.

31 — Finished new roof on the house.

1918

Jan. 8 — River open as far as can be seen. Health very poor.

12 — Lynx moving down river one or two a night; no chance to catch them.

15 — Goats moving out of reach. Using canoe on the river.

16 — One lynx. Weather getting mild.

20 — Rain today.

22 — One lynx.

28 — One goat; been cold for a few days.

Feb. 1 — Cold weather nearly all month of January. Lynx robbed my meat cache up the river. Salt and tea once a day. Gradually getting weaker.

5 — Colder weather; feeling very bad. Just able to take care of myself.

10 — Milder weather, feeling very bad. Heavy fall of snow.

15 — Good weather continues; feeling some better.

24 — More snow. Living on dry meat and tallow.

26 — Shot one goat from the river.

Mar. 2 — Shot one goat.

11 — Starting for Dry Bay, believing the river open. Out about one hour, struck the ice; can't go either way; too weak to haul the canoe. Snow soft; no game here.

25 — Trying to get to the house. River is frozen in places and rising. The sleigh now only three miles from there, but open river and perpendicular cliffs keep me from getting any farther. At present cannot find anything to eat here. Eyes are getting bad.

28 — Eyes can't stand the sun at all. Finest kind of weather.

Apr. 1 — Got to the house with what I could carry. Wolverines had been there eating my skins, robes and moccasins, old meat and also my goat skin door. They tried to run me last night; came through the stovepipe hole, showing fight. Heavy fall of snow. Canoe and some traps down river about five miles close to Indian grave mark. Camp about half-ways.

3 — Still snowing. Cooking my last grub; no salt; no tea.

4 — Shot one goat, using all but three of my shells. Can't see the sight at all.

7 — Wolverines working on camp below, carrying away my things. Ate part of my bearskin pants. Packed the old .30-30 out into the brush. Eyes are getting worse again; don't even stand the snow.

10 — Wolverines ate my bedding and one snowshoe. In the tent — getting shaky in the legs. A five-mile walk a big day's work.

12 — Seen a fox track today. Birds are coming, too. Fine weather.

15 — The no-salt diet hitting me pretty hard. Eyes are getting worse; in the bunk most of the time.

17 — Rain yesterday and today.

20 — Finest weather continues again; cooking the last grub; got to stay in the bunk most of the time; my legs won't carry me very far.

My eyes useless for hunting; the rest of my body also useless. I believe my time has come. My belongings —everything I got — I give to Jos. Pellerine of Dry Bay; if not alive to Paul Swartzkopf, Alesk River. April 22, 1918.

(signed)   V. Swanson

This is the statement of a man found dead in his cabin by Barry Trefgar and myself on the 18th day of August, 1918.

(signed)   Fred Zastrow.

Doug Peacock has spent a score of years photographing grizzlies at very close range. He suggests that if you are confronted by a bear, you should remain still, inoffensive and yet defensive. Don't make sudden movements or loud noises. Don't holler or wave or, worst of all, run. Stand your ground, arms outstretched to make yourself appear bigger. Keep your head turned to the side; don't look the grizzly in the eye; talk to the bear. The bear will either turn aside or allow you to slowly back away. Using this method, Peacock has survived situations with bears that came within a few feet of him.

Try the scare method if confronted by a grizzly. Wave your hands, shout, shoot a gun in the air. This tactic has been used successfully by many people (especially when confronted by sub-adult bears). It frequently does not work with a grizzly sow and her cubs.

A grizzly is walking toward you, and a tree is only a few steps away. Climb it, going up at least 35 feet. If you've unsuccessfully tried the Peacock method/or scare tactics on a female grizzly with cubs and she knocks you over, play dead. If you're ever taken from a tent at night, this bear thinks you're dinner. Scream and fight back. (September 91, p.40)

Grizzly bear
(about 8 ft. long)

The prairie rattler, found throughout the western U.S. and southwestern Canada grows to five feet. It is a daytime hunter of rodents, so watch your step.
(August 96, p. 23)

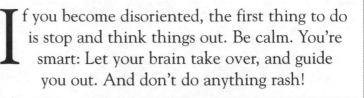

If you become disoriented, the first thing to do is stop and think things out. Be calm. You're smart: Let your brain take over, and guide you out. And don't do anything rash!

In an emergency, spread a tarp to catch as much rain as possible. Raise corners so water runs into a receptacle. (March 94, p.47)

When playing the survival game, set up your shelter (tube tent) in a spot that is out of the wind and rain. Put on your cold weather clothing. Make a mattress of pine boughs, get into your shelter, wrap up in the space blanket (silver side in), and relax. Eat a granola bar or two, and wait for morning. (November 95, p.89)

If we've done our homework, in the literal sense of the word, things done at home before venturing into the field, we'll feel more comfortable dealing with situations others find frightening and that may have frightened us. Remember, if we have enough clothing to survive the weather and have baselines to which we can walk within a few days, we'll be okay; no one starves to death in a few days. (March 92, p.65)

Traditionally, there are distress signals of all kinds (dots, dashes). Dashes are issued in threes to distinguish them from normal or random activities.

During daylight, smoke is an excellent short- and long-range attention getter. A single plume of thick smoke can be enough to attract attention, especially if rescuers are looking for you, but once again, three separate and distinct plumes send a more emphatic message. On clear days, white smoke generated by piling moist wood, leaves, and grasses onto the flame is most easily seen. In overcast weather, dark smoke made by burning oily rags or any kind of rubber if available is preferred. As with all visual signaling, the effect is enhanced if you're able to send up your signals form comparatively open and preferably elevated terrain. (September 01, p.36)

Take an extra 1000 calories (above and beyond food for the trip). It will provide back-up energy for walking out in an emergency and internal heat for sitting up or sleeping through the night. One thousand calories is four Milky Way bars. Carry a water bottle in the winter, to prevent dehydration.

Spending a night in a space blanket and eating chocolate to keep warm is adequate but not always ideal. To improve your comfort and morale, as well as stacking the odds in your favor it there's a bad storm, carry either waterproof matches or a few lighters in the event that the vegetation and weather permit building a fire. (March 92, p.65)

You survived the night, now in the morning make your self large. Set up signals. Put fluorescent orange navigation tape everywhere. Stomp SOS into the snow or grass. Lay out the aluminum foil. Get a fire going and heap on green bought for smoke signals. Keep the fire going at night, if possible not only for heat, but because search aircraft will be able to spot it from miles away. Blow your whistle every few minutes whenever you're away.

When you are lost and in need of water if water is close at hand, fill your bottle and add the purification tablets. Melt snow if necessary, but again, add purification tablets. If water is plentiful, drink often, and more than you think you'll need. If you have a fire going, warm the water before you drink it. (September 92, p.89)

If you're hunting with a group and get separated, try the backwoods method. It will work only with shotguns. Open the breech of the shotgun, regardless of the type. Remove all shells and leave the breech open. Turn the gun around and place the muzzle tightly to your lips and blow as if it were a trumpet. You should get a high note at first and finish off with a lower note as the pressure falls off. This method was originally used to call fox or coon hounds when the hunter had no proper horn. You will be surprised how far the sound will carry. Remember: Clean moisture from the bore of the gun. (October 92, p.83)

One of the surest ways to avoid getting lost in strange country is to look back often as you enter new areas. What you see when you look back is what you see coming back this same way. As you enter strange country you may be walking downhill. When you return the same route, you will be looking and walking uphill, facing an entirely different terrain than the one you saw when you set out. This is one of the original tricks of experienced woodsmen. (October 92, p.79)

Your brain can usually sort out an outdoor emergency, whatever it may be, if you let it. Panic however, is an overpowering emotion that often short-circuits rational behavior. Your goal must be to prevent panic from taking control, and you begin that battle now. "Don't panic" is a near-worthless admonition when it surfaces after the fact. Program, educate and brainwash yourself continually, in advance of any emergency, so you can handle anything. Play that game of "what if" with respect to outdoor crises before they arise. (May 93, p.54)

A shade shelter in open desert. It may be difficult to find protection from the hot sun. A tarp, a Space Blanket or even a garment (poncho, jacket, shirt) can be rigged fly-style with a center pole and guylines. Or you can stack rocks to elevate and anchor the tarp or garment. (July 95, p.75)

The most basic deadfall trap is the figure-four configuration, which is easily made with a pocketknife. Note that the trigger stick must be sharpened to skewer and securely hold the bait. The best fall object is a heavy, flat-bottomed stone, though a large log will also work on small animals. Equally important is a firm base area; a flat stone is best. Lacking that, you can use a perching base, such as a low rock or log, onto which the animal must climb to seize the bait. For trapping rodents, you can bait the trigger stick simply by rubbing the sharp end alongside your nose, where skin oils gather; better still (if you have it) is a bit of human food such as bread, peanut butter, margarine or cheese. (July 95, p.73)

The simple snare. The noose for this easily constructed trap is best made with thin, strong wire, though you can use propped-open fishing line in an emergency, preferably stronger than 15-pound-test. Set your snares (as many as you can make) along the prey's runways and travel routes. Best of all are bottleneck sites, where the animal is forced to run into the snare, having little opportunity to go around it. You can improve natural bottlenecks by fencing off possible detours with logs, rocks or other native materials. (July 95, p.73)

In an emergency situation, the ability to build a fire could prove to be your most important survival skill. When planning a cold-weather hunt, always carry a firestarting kit for extra insurance. (February 01, p.17)

Captured by the Indians

By Nelson Lee

Nelson Lee's account of spending three years as a prisoner of the Comanche Indian tribe in the 1850s brought national attention to the suffering endured by white captives. Lee's saga began when he joined a group of twenty men planning to drive a herd of horses from Texas to California. As a former Texas Ranger, Lee knew the dangers inherent in such a trip. After a few days on the trail, a band of Comanches attacked the camp and killed all but four men. The

Indians slowly and brutally tortured to death two of the men while forcing Lee and his companion to watch. The other survivor was then carried off to a separate encampment, never to be seen again. Lee survived due to his offhand purchase of a fancy pocket watch before the trip. His ability to make the object ring on command made the Indians believe he possessed some sort of magic.

Lee endured some horrific treatment during his years of being traded from band to band among the Comanches, but soon after he was forced to take a wife by a chief named Rolling Thunder he finally found an opportunity to make a run for it.

AFTER LEAVING THE VOLCANIC VALLEY and ascertaining the feeding grounds of the bison, we returned to the village, and soon again set forth on the yearly buffalo hunt. It is a singular fact that on these excursions the hunters are followed by droves of wolves. They seem to have an instinctive knowledge of the business in which the party is about to engage. As soon as the skin is stripped from the buffalo, they surround the carcass and devour it. To wake in the dead of night, after dreaming, peradventure of early home and friends, to find yourself under a rude tent, in those far distance wilds, surrounded by a savage tribe, produces sensations, lonely and desolate indeed, but terror mingles with the sense of desolation, when all around, the adjacent solitudes are vocal with the barking and snarling and howling of wolves, gorging themselves at their midnight feasts.

It was at such times as these my soul longed to reach once more the abodes of civilized man. Though greatly discouraged, I have entirely despaired of sooner or later effecting an escape. Aside from the charm which still lingered around the watch, the silver child of the sun, that had so providentially shielded me from unspeakable outrage during the earlier portion of my captivity, I was confident the covenant of blood into which I had entered, and more than all, my marriage with Sleek Otter, would henceforth save me from violence.

At this time I had no apprehensions whatever in regard to my personal safety, so long as I remained an obedient captive, fulfilling the humble duties imposed upon me. A detected attempted at escape, however, I was fully aware, would be followed by the severest penalties. I had so long, and so intensely, contemplated the subject, that there was no possible aspect in which it could present itself, that had not received the closest and most careful scrutiny and consideration. Of one thing I had become thoroughly convinced, which was, that if I had been successful in escaping from the tribe of the Spotted Leopard, without the means of killing game, or making a fire, I should, most assuredly, have perished from starvation among the mountains.

It became necessary, therefore, to devise some plan by which, in case the opportunity offered, I could provide myself with these indispensable conveniences. It is probable I could, on many occasions, have reached the mountains unperceived, after the marriage, and the attempt been made, but it was utterly impossible to have done so, providing myself, at the same time, with any kind of arms,—the watchfulness over me in respect to them, being strict and constant.

It was while indulging in these never-ending speculations that The Rolling Thunder ordered me to saddle my mule and accompany him on a long journey.

His destination was a village three days' journey to the north. At this place a general convention had been called, to be composed of all the chiefs of all the different tribes inhabiting the country between the northern bounds of Mexico and the regions of perpetual snow. The object of the convention was to induce the Indian nations, hitherto at variance, to bury the hatchet as between themselves, smoke the peace pipe, and unite in a universal bond of brotherhood, for the purpose of preventing the whites from passing through their territories to the settlements on the Pacific coast.

It was, as I then understood it, and now believe, to enter into an alliance, with the view of waging an exterminating and implacable war, upon every train of emigrants or other party, moving towards California, Oregon, The Great Salt Lake, or any other point in either of those directions. How it terminated, circumstances unanticipated, but of a most exciting and stirring character forbid my knowing, yet, that the design was precisely such as I have mentioned, is a fact, which I beg all those who contemplate making the overland route, to bear seriously in mind.

The Rolling Thunder, before taking his departure, arrayed himself with extraordinary care. A dozen scalps were attached to his war shirt; silver trinkets representing the moon in all its phases, were fastened on his breast; his feet were clad in new and cunningly embroidered moccasins, and on his head rested a crown of feathers plucked from the crow, the kingfisher, the prairie hen and the eagle, so dyed by his ingenious wives as to reflect all the colors of the rainbow. Of all the horses that grazed the wide pastures round about his camp, he was mounted upon the most fleet and spirited—the weapons of war in which he was accoutred, were a knife thrust through his belt, a hatchet suspended from the pommel of his saddle, and a Mexican rifle, rare among his tribe, upon the possession of which, he prided himself exceedingly.

I bestrode the same old mule that had so often and so far borne me on her back, with nothing hanging from my saddlebow but a huge buffalo horn, wherewith to furnish my doughty master with cool draughts from the streams, as we journeyed on the way. Saluting the Sleek Otter, who little thought it was the last nod she would ever receive from her long-haired spouse—for, not having seen a razor for three years, I was very far from being "the man all shaven and shorn, who married the maiden all forlorn"—we trotted away from the village, myself in advance, neither of us destined ever to return.

From early morning we traveled leisurely but steadily and at sunset entered a valley wherein resided a small tribe, whose chief was Nis-ti-u-na, the Wild Horse. The usual hospitalities were extended—or rather on this occasion they were unusual—inasmuch as a party had just returned from a meeting with the traders, bringing with them a quantity of muscal, a kind of whiskey, distilled from the fruit of a tree, commonly known in Mexico as the cabbage tree.

An Indian's dignity, whether chief or subject, never rises to that elevated degree which prevents his getting drunk every opportunity that offers, and consequently it followed, as a matter of course, that so distinguished a visitor as The Rolling Thunder, arriving at that peculiar juncture, could not avoid stretching himself on this buffalo skin that night without a weighty "brick in his hat." In other words, the sedate old fellow became beastly intoxicated, —forgot altogether the decorum that characterized his customary walk and conversation—vainly attempted to be funny—danced out of place—and whooped when there was no occasion for it—in fact, was as boisterous and silly as about half a gallon of bad whiskey could make him.

However, bright and early in the morning, the chief was again on his proper legs, ready to set forward on the journey, intending to lodge that night at another village further to the north. After a breakfast of mustang steak, which rested ill on his sour stomach, we bade the sore-haired sons of the tribe of the Wild Horse good morning, and pursued our travel. Very soon we passed out of their valley and entered the defiles of the mountains. The last night's debauch had set the old chief on fire, and before the sun had half way ascended to the zenith, his throat was parched, and he was mad with thirst. But there was no water to be found. On and on we went, threading our way through thick bushes, around the sharp points of overhanging cliffs, across rough and rugged ravines, but nowhere did a spring or running stream greet his longing eyes. We continued to press forward, in this manner until about one o'clock in the afternoon, when, reaching the bottom of a deep hollow, we discovered water oozing from the base of a perpendicular precipice, and trickling down a little muddy channel through the grass.

He called, impetuously, upon me to fill the horn at once. Though I attempted to obey his order with all possible celerity, the rill was so extremely shallow, that in spite of my best endeavors, every dip I made, the contents of the horn would come up in the proportion of three parts mud to one of water. Perceiving the difficulty, he leaped from his horse, directing me to hold him by the bridle, threw his Mexican rifle on the ground, and laying down upon it in the grass, thrust his scorched lips into the little stream.

Standing by the horse's side, I observed the hatchet hanging from the pommel of the saddle. The thought flashed through my mind quick as the fierce lightning, that the hour of my deliverance had come, at last, and snatching it, in that instant from its place, I leaped towards him, burying the dull edge a broad hand's breadth in his brain. A moment sufficed to draw the rifle from beneath him, jerk the long knife from his girdle, mount his horse, and dash wildly away over an unknown path, towards the land of freedom.

Turning about, I retraced the path we had followed, some two miles, remembering to have seen a narrow defile stretching to the west, as we passed along. Plunging into this I spurred on at a breakneck pace, over piles of broken stones that had rolled down from the declivities, penetrated barricades of tangled thorns and brushwood, the mule all the while following closely at the horse's heels, and at the end of six miles, encountered a bold bluff extending entirely across the western termination of the ravine, abruptly arresting any further progress in that direction. This bluff was the eastern side of a high, bleak, rocky spur, which shot out from a still more elevated range, right athwart the path I was pursuing. Wheeling northward, and moving along its base, I reached, at length, a contracted crevice, half filled with broken, shar-angled fragments of rock, up which, with great difficulty, myself, horse and mule managed to clamber, until we gained a comparatively level spot, a kind of terrace, some twenty feet wide, about half way to the summit. Further ascent was impossible and no other recourse was left, but to follow the terrace whithersoever it led. Its surface presented, as an Indian would term it, a clear trail, and was, undoubtedly, one of the paths traversed by deer and other animals while migrating from one feeding ground to another. We followed it, as it wound around the southern declivity of the precipice, becoming more and more narrow as we advanced, until, to my unutterable horror, it had contracted to a width, less than two feet. A sharp point round which it circled just in front of me, hid the view beyond, but all appearances indicated it terminated there. On one side were great, loose overhanging rocks impossible to ascend and threatening to fall, on the other, an almost perpendicular descent of at least a hundred feet. The horse hesitated to proceed, as if conscious of the danger to which he was exposed.—Between the wall of adamant on the right, and the precipice on the left, there was not sufficient room to enable either horse or mule to turn around, and so entirely did their bodies fill up the path, it was impracticable for me to turn back, had it become necessary so to do, without pushing the poor brutes down the fearful steep.

With eyes turned away from the dizzy depth below, down

which, in my despair, a strange impulse urged me to plunge, and end a miserable life at once, I crawled carefully to the sharp point before me, closely hugging the upper side, and peering round it, beheld with ineffable satisfaction, that it expanded into a broad, smooth road. Much urging and coaxing, finally succeeded in inducing the horse to pass the point of danger. My sense of relief, when we had reached a place of safety was like that of the awakened sleeper when he thanks God the awful chasm over which he has been hanging by a slender twig, is but the vagary of a dream.

From the spot now gained I gazed broad upon the surrounding scene, and a wilder or more dreary one never broke upon my vision. On all sides, around and above, were piled mountain upon mountain as far as the eye could reach. Here and there, among the defiles, could be discovered strips of timber, but the summits, as they appeared in the distance, were bare and rock, their bald peaks stretching to the clouds.

After some examination, for I was in too great haste to linger, a narrow opening in a south west direction attracted my attention, and towards it I turned my steps. The descent, though not entirely impracticable, was tedious in the extreme. The ledges were numerous and abrupt, and difficult to pass, often drawing me far out of a straight course. Finally, however, the opening was reached, proving to be another ravine averaging two hundred yards in width, over which were scattered cedar trees, and clusters of thick bushes. By the time I had reached the southwestern termination of this little solitary valley, the sun had set, and darkness was fast spreading over the earth. Pushing into the centre of a dense thicket, covering, perhaps, two or three acres, the loneliest spot that presented itself, I halted for the night.

Securing the horse to a limb by the bridle, and removing the buffalo skin saddle, I sat down upon and consulted with myself as to what it was best to do. My safety depended much upon circumstances. If the body of the chief should happen to be discovered immediately, my escape was doubtful. The moment it was found, my knowledge of savage life taught me, a party would instantly and eagerly start upon my trail, and, at the same time messengers be sent to all the tribes far and near, calling on them to keep a sharp lookout for my approach, so that I had as much to apprehend in front as in the rear.

I was provided with the dead chief's rifle and ammunition, and consequently had the means of kindling a fire, but making the one or discharging the other, at least, for some days, would be a dangerous experiment, inasmuch as the noise of the rifle, or the light of the fire might expose me. The demands of appetite, however, would render it necessary to risk both, and in fact, already were they becoming clamorous, having fasted since our early departure in the morning from the camp of the Wild Horse. Being impossible at that hour to capture game, my thoughts turned upon the mule. She had followed me unexpectedly, and could be of no possible use, on the contrary, in all probability would prove an annoyance. Necessity, which is, indeed, the mother of invention, suggested how I could turn her to account, and the suggestion was adopted. Walking up to the tired and patient beast, as unsuspicious of harm as was her now stark owner when he bent down to drink, I grasped the long knife that was wont to grace his girdle, and drew it across her throat.

When life was extinct, I cut from her hams long thin strips of flesh to the measure of some ten pounds, and having done so, resolved to run the venture of kindling a fire, trusting that the Rolling Thunder was still reposing undiscovered and undisturbed, where I had left him. Accordingly I gathered a pile of sticks, and withdrawing the charge from the rifle, ignited a priming of power which presently resulted in a ruddy, and under other circumstances, a cheerful blaze. The mule meat was then broiled, and satisfying present appetite upon a portion, the remainder was carefully laid aside for future necessity. Then provided with provisions for several days to come, it occurred to me that I might suffer for the lack of water, on those thirsty mountains. The buffalo horn, though convenient at a stream or spring, could not be used in carrying away their contents. Some kind of vessel was indispensable, and in order to be furnished with such an article, I cut the bladder from the mule, blew it up, dried it by the fire, filled from a sluggish pool at hand, tying the mouth with a strong buffalo string.

These labors performed, with the reloaded rifle in my hands, I sat down on the buffalo skin at the foot of a cedar tree, and leaned against its truck. Here, a new terror awaited me I had not anticipated. The mule's blood had been scented by wild beasts, wolves and panthers, which began to scream. Nearer and nearer they approached until the horse snuffed and snorted, and I could hear their teeth snap, and the dry sticks crackle beneath their feet. A dozen times I was on the point of ascending the tree, momentarily expecting to be attacked. With such a crash would they break through the thicket that many times I bounded to my feet, thinking the Indians were upon me. It was a fearful night, and the most fearful sound that has ever fallen on my ears is the scream of the panther, so like is it to the plaintive, agonizing shriek of a human being. The fortunate resolution I had taken to build a fire, undoubtedly kept them off, and the absence of Indians beyond the sound of their unearthly confusion was the sole cause of my hiding place not being disclosed. It taught me, however, a lesson not thenceforward to be forgotten, that is to say, never to encamp where I had killed my game.

In the morning, very early, I proceeded on the journey, and in the course of half an hour was again intercepted by another mountain. It was high noon when I reached the summit, so rough and difficult was the ascent. Often, having entered a gully whose entrance allured me with the promise of a favorable path, I would break through dense thickets of prickly pear, the thorns piercing and tearing my flesh, until thinking I was about to emerge upon the plateau above, a wall of fallen stone, or the trunk of a prostrate tree, would suddenly present an invincible barrier, compelling me to return down the same painful path, and seek, in another place, some more feasible passage.

During the afternoon, I kept my course, as near as possible, along the ridge of the highlands, but notwithstanding I improved every moment of the time, so rugged was the route, it is probable I had not passed ten miles in a direct line from the place of departure in the morning, when night again overtook me. This was passed under a ledge, in a little nook where a portion of the rock, in the form of a wedge, has fallen out. On such an eminence as this it would have been madness to light a fire—nothing less than a signal to any in pursuit to come up and take me—nevertheless, the tough mule meat, and the yet unemptied bladder, furnished me with a thankful repast. My poor horse, however, was not so well supplied, there being neither water or grass here, and but few bushes on which to browse. Wrapping the buffalo skin around me I endeavored to sleep, realizing the invigoration it would bring was necessary to sustain the fatigue and hardship before me; but my slumbers were broken and troubled, full of fearful dreams, in which I was clambering over rocks, or pursued by Indians, yelling close on my trail, and yet, unable to fly, having lost the power to move, so that I arose with the first faint glimpse of the rising sun, sore and unrefreshed.

I continued along the height a portion of this day, and would have pursued it further, deeming it safer than a less elevated path, had it now become absolutely necessary to find water for the horse. This necessity induced me to make my way down the mountain side, a labor I succeeded in achieving towards the close of the day, when I struck a green delicious valley, a mile wide in some parts, on which wild horses, a few buffalo, deer, and antelope were grazing, and which apparently stretched a long distance to the south. Fearing to adventure upon it in daylight, I hid in a cedar copse until dark, when allowing the horse to slake his thirst at a rivulet, and feed an hour on the rank grass, I mounted and rode as fast as I could urge him until long after midnight, keeping in the shadows of the mountains. I had ridden in this manner, at least, thirty miles, congratulating myself on the rapid progress I was making, when the little valley came to a point, shut in by impassable precipices.

The opening day disclosed that I had been completely entrapped. The valley was surrounded on all sides by precipitous rocks, up which, in some places, I might possibly have made my way along, but which it was beyond the power of the horse to ascend. My situation now became unpleasant, it being probable that a luxuriant valley like this, abounding in game, and so rarely to be found amidst these sterile regions, must be frequented by Indians.

No alternative presented itself, but to turn back and retrace, cautiously, the course over which I had galloped with so much satisfaction the previous night. The whole of this day was occupied in traveling about fifteen miles. Along the south side of the valley, which I was now coursing, at the average distance from each other, of three-fourths of a mile, perhaps, narrow points or promontories shot out from the side of the mountains, the space of prairie land lying between them resembling a half-moon or segment of a circle. From the extremity of one of these headlands I would reconnoitre, until satisfied the "coast was clear," then dash across to the next as fast as the horse could run. In this manner, as before stated, some fifteen miles were accomplished which brought me to the close of the day, and also to a path that opened a comparatively easy passage up the steep. For two days I wandered over these mountains, rising constantly from ridge to ridge until the summit was attained and passed, and at evening of the sixth day of the flight descended into a dark, cavernous defile where I found a spring of water, and many deer browsing around it. The mule meat, besides being so tough as to demand the exercise of my utmost powers of mastication, was now nearly gone. Here, for the first time I discharged the rifle, bringing down a plump doe, whose skin and hind quarters I carried forward four or five miles and halted for the night, leaving the remainder as an entertainment for the wolves. Selecting a secluded spot under an overhanging cliff, and approached through a thick growth of brushwood, I kindled, for the second time, a fire, and prepared a meal of venison. Though unsalted and unpeppered, and without the concomitants of currant jelly or other dessert, after the hard fare upon which I had so long existed, no epicure ever enjoyed with a keener relish the daintiest dish, than I did, slice after slice, of the juicy and tender steaks. Venison will remain in a state of preservation longer than the flesh of any animal with which I am acquainted. Notwithstanding the weather was warm, I was not obliged after this to shoot a deer oftener than once in three days.

The seventh day found me toiling over a succession of mountains smoother, and of more grand ascent, than any I had yet crossed. My course here led in a southwest direction, having conceived the idea, which subsequently proved very erroneous, that it would conduct me to the Mexican State of Chihuahua. At length, arriving at the heighth of land, a wide prairie unexpectedly spread out before me, over which numerous Indian horsemen were riding, and at my feet stood an Indian town of at least three hundred tents.

The prairie extended to the west farther than I could perceive, but the mountains that bounded its eastern terminus were distinguishable at a distance, as near as I could estimate, of twenty miles. Anxious to escape, at once, from so dangerous a vicinity I lost no time in coming to a resolution, which was to make the detour of its eastern extremity. In order to do so, however, it was necessary again to retrace my steps many rough and weary miles; but perseverance, incited by an apprehension of immediate danger, enabled me to "overcome all things," insomuch that late in the evening of the day following the discovery of the town, I had rounded the point of the prairie and was encamped in a snug and solitary fastness of the mountains that lined its western side. Until I passed far beyond this Indian settlement I exercised the same caution as if assured intelligence had been conveyed to them of the death of Rolling Thunder, and as if I knew they were on the watch for my approach.

For nearly two weeks now I was lost in a vast range of mountains, sometimes going forward, at others compelled to turn back, winding through deep hollows, and climbing over abrupt precipices, often suffering with hunger and parched with thirst. I doubt if civilized or savage man ever before or since made the passage of this sterile region. During the day I directed my course by the sun, always keeping in view, as far as practicable, in my zig-zag progress some prominent peak far in the distance. At night I was guided by the north star. However, there were many cloudy days and nights, during which I was unable to proceed with certainty, and consequently lost much time.

There were many difficulties, hardships and dangers encountered on this lonesome journey, a correct description whereof it is impossible for me to draw, or the reader to conceive. For instance, I was frightfully annoyed by snakes. It has been seen on a former page that the sight of these reptiles always inspired me with emotions of dread and terror. There was a flat-headed adder I frequently discovered on wet ground and near streams and springs of water; rattlesnakes were everywhere; but there was another species, a kind I had never seen, and am ignorant of the name naturalists have applied to it. It was of a brown color, rather slim, and as often exceeding as falling short of nine feet in length. It inhabited the clefts of the rocks, and stretched itself out on the ledges in the sun. One of its peculiar characteristics was to blow, when disturbed, emitting a loud, disagreeable, unnatural noise, half hiss, half bellow.—Frequently while laboring up the steep side of a mountain, drawing myself up a declivity by grasping slight root twigs that had sprung up in the cracks and crevices of the rocks, as my head emerged above the surface I was striving to attain, one of these monsters would raise itself to the height of three feet and blow directly in my face. It made my "locks," which, indeed, was "knotted and combined, to part, and each particular hair to stand on end." Bears were numerous, and occasionally a panther could be seen stealing noiselessly through the underwood, but these cause me little, in fact, no apprehension whatever.

On the twentieth day Indians were again discovered. I had reached another valley early in the morning, and from a secure point was making observations, when I perceived them, to the number of a hundred horsemen, followed by a train of pack mules moving towards the west. There was no village to be seen, and I concluded, therefore, they were a party on a visit to some neighboring tribe, the buffalo hunting season having passed.

Watching them until the last one had disappeared, and making myself certain others were not approaching, I hurried over the narrow valley at a rapid pace, and commenced another "crossing of the Alps."

By this time, the horse had suffered so much from thirst and the want of forage, that he had become emaciated in the extreme. His hoofs, likewise, were worn out; my feet covered with bruises, and my whole body sore and stiff. In this condition we reached, one day, a singular spot, a deep basin among the hills, enclosing bottom land to the extent of ten or fifteen acres, covered alternately with patches of grass and thickets of brush and wholly shut in by lofty eminences. A spring, clear as crystal, gushed from the base of the mountain on one side, and a number of deer were feeding at different points. At this green spot in the desert I remained twelve days.

Though I had no mirror with me to make a particular examination, I expect my personal appearance was not especially attractive. Three years had elapsed since my beard, or the hair of my head had defiled a comb, brush, or razor. My moccasins were dilapidated beyond redemption, my leggings and hunting shirt in shreds, torn in a thousand places by thorns and brambles. I still retained the deer skin hank which bound my head and fastened on the forehead with a clasp, preventing the hair from falling over my eyes, but the little painted feathers with which the Sleek Otter had ambitiously adorned it, were long since blown to the winds of heaven.

My employments during the twelve days I halted in this solitary place were various. The most laborious portion of each day was spent in ascending one or the other of the adjacent peaks, and taking an observation of the surrounding region, in order to ascertain if an enemy was approaching. With much difficulty I cleared a small space in the centre of the densest thicket, cutting out and pulling up the roots, whereon I erected a fireplace of stone, the object of taking so much pains being, to kindle the fire where the thick shrubbery about it would, in a great measure, conceal the light. Here I went assiduously at work to provide for a "rainy day," in the matter of provisions, and to replenish my wardrobe. I shot four or five deer at different times, drying as much of the flesh as I deemed it convenient to carry and manufacturing the skins into necessary articles of wearing apparel. The only tool I possessed was a knife, but with this managed to accomplish all I undertook. The moccasins were made of the hide while in its green state, applied to the foot with the hair inside, fastened with stout whangs of the same materials inserted through holes made with the point of the knife and tied, and left in that condition to dry. I was familiar with the Indian mode of dressing buckskin with the brains of the deer itself, and had no difficulty in preparing new leggings and hunting coat. Perhaps the fit was not admirable, nor the suit, taken as a whole, such as would be commended by a fashionable man at a select party, nevertheless, it suited the society with which I was then associating, and was extremely comfortable. I delayed several days after these arrangements were effected on account of the horse, which notwithstanding he had plenty of pasture and water, did not seem to recruit; but, on the contrary, to be effectually broken down.

However, I set out again at the end of twelve days, arrayed in my new clothes, and with the bundle of dried venison hanging at the saddle bow, wildly imagining myself in the neighborhood of Santa Fe. My course now led over a mountainous region, if possible, more difficult, barren and desolate than any that had preceded it. Water was rarely to be found, and in many parts there was not sufficient grass on a thousand acres to supply the horse with one night's provender. He constantly became more and more tender footed and lame, the flesh had departed from his bones, and the proud and fiery spirit with which he had pranced out of his native valley, amidst the salutations of the tribe, with the Rolling Thunder on his back, was gone—completely gone. I was now compelled to lead him, stopping frequently for him to lie down. At length, the supply of water I had brought with me from the last spring was exhausted, and I was obliged to leave him on the mountains.

Rolling up the buffalo skin inclosing my drinking horn and other articles, and tying it with the bridle reins into the form of a knapsack, I threw it upon my back, shouldered the rifle, and bidding the poor horse a sorrowful farewell, started on alone.

Now for the first time my heart died within me. For aught I could discover the abodes of civilised men were as far off as when I began the long and tedious journey. I began to doubt myself, to fear that I had become crazed and lost, and instead of pursuing the southwesterly course I imagined, was only wandering round and round over the same everlasting solitudes. Moreover, since parting from the horse who had been as a companion to me, whose presence during the silent hours of the night, stamping and feeding round me, seemed like a protection, I was lonesome and desolate indeed. And I was sick in body as well as soul. My limbs had become swollen and the wounds and bruises that covered me inflamed and painful.

In this condition of body and mind, several days after my leaving the horse, I came upon a fountain of pure water, gushing out beautifully from a rock. The cool draught was so refreshing and its application to my burning body afforded so much relief, I fully resolved to proceed no further, but there linger through the remainder of my life, which seemed fast waning to its close. A night's rest, however, relieved me somewhat of pain, inspired me with renewed hopes, and animated me to make another attempt to drag myself wearily along. But day by day I grew weaker as I advanced, the vigorous strength and hardy constitution with which Providence had blessed me, breaking down under these incessant struggles and privations.

Very often while reclining on the ground, my feet resting on some little elevation to relieve pain, it seemed certain that sufficient energy would not return to permit me rise again, and still more often I prayed God that when I fell asleep I might never wake again.

The fifty-sixth day of my distressing travels brought me to a rolling prairie of considerable extent, dotted with many small groves of timber. Into one of these I had made my way to avoid the hot beams of the sun, and was lying in the shade, in a drowsy, half sleeping state, when I was startled by the sharp crack of a rifle close at hand. My first thought was: is it possible they have chased me so far? Bounding to my feet, I held the rifle in my hands, ready to bring it to an aim as soon as necessity required, resolving, weak as I was, after such incredible suffering to stand on the defense. In the course of some ten minutes, instead of being rushed upon by a band of Indians, a mounted Mexican, wearing a wide-brimmed sombrero, came riding leisurely along, with a deer which had received its death wound from the discharge that had so astounded me, thrown over his horse's back, behind the saddle.

"How do you do?" he exclaimed, in mongrel Spanish, and much astonished.

Not knowing the character of the company into which I had so unexpectedly fallen, and deeming it prudent for safety to conceal my true story for the present, I walked up to him and addressing him in his own language, with which I am familiar, replied, 'Sick and dying, will you help me, my friend?"

"How came you here?" he inquired.

"I have been lost among the mountains," I answered "and have been trying to make my way to the settlements."

Much other conversation ensued, when he informed me he was one of a party of three who had been on a trading expedition to the Apaches, and were now on their return—that his companions were encamped not far distant—that they belonged to San Fernandez, below Eagle Pass, near the Rio Grande, and concluded by inviting me to accompany him to the camp. Perceiving how difficult it was for me to proceed, he dismounted and helped me into the saddle and walked by the side of the horse, conversing kindly, and evidently much interested in my behalf.

His companions were cooking when we arrived and like himself, were greatly astonished at beholding me. However, they gave me a hospitable and generous welcome, exhibiting the true spirit of the Good Samaritan. In their train were eight pack mules, loaded with buffalo robes and furs, the proceeds of their traffic with the tribes. Their kindness won my entire confidence at once, and without further hesitation I related the whole story of my adventures. The interest my previous story of being lost among the mountains had excited was vastly enhanced by this disclosure, and no pains were now spared to administer to my comfort and convenience. The eight packs were rearranged so as to afford me one of the mules to ride, and we started on.

The third day we crossed the Rio Grande upon a raft, swimming the mules and horses, and passing through a number of frontier settlements, at all of which my misfortunes were related by the traders, and followed by the kindest treatment. On the seventh day thereafter, we entered the town of San Fernandez. The names of these humane and generous men are Antonio Halleno, Josef de Silva and Mario Francisco des Lezzez. I owe them a lasting debt of gratitude which I can only repay by proclaiming their noble hearted generosity to a poor suffering wanderer among the mountains wherever this narrative may go.

I remained six weeks at San Fernandez under the care of a physician, at the end of which time Josef de Silva accompanied me to Matamoras. From thence I proceeded to Brazos Santiago and shipped for Havana, where having fulfilled my parting promise to Aikens to communicate the intelligence of his fate, in case I escaped, to his friend at Corpus Christi, I set sail in the schooner Elizabeth Jones, Capt. William Hudson, and on the 10th day of November, 1858, reached the United States.

You can closely approximate your maximum heart rate by subtracting your age from 220. Only those in excellent physical condition should approach their maximum heart rate, and only for a short period. Most physicians would not have you work at a rate exceeding 75 percent of your maximum. Calculating your heart rate while afield is quick and easy, and a smart thing to do. Simply take your pulse for 15 seconds and multiply this figure by four. (June 95, p.65)

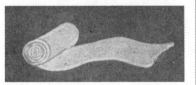

A person can die or go into fatal shock after only a few minutes of heavy blood loss. The best method is direct pressure to the wound, preferably over an application of sterile gauze. If gauze isn't available, use clean cloth of any kind; lacking that, use the flat of your hand. Apply continuous pressure—don't dab or lift the dressing to check blood flow. With wounds to the arms or legs, it may help to elevate the limb and/or splint to prevent clot-disruptive motion. Tourniquets should be used only in cases of extreme injury such as gunshot wounds or amputations, since they completely stop blood flow, killing the tissue. Even a briefly applied tourniquet can cause permanent nerve and vessel damage. (July 95, p.77)

The two-hand carry is a good technique when transporting an injured person—Rescuers grasp wrists to form a seat with their hands and support unconscious victim's upper body with free arms. The four-hand carry is for conscious victims only. (August 95, p. 54)

Train yourself to observe mountains, cliffs, draws, canyons, swamps, creeks, rivers, trails —any clues to your route—and to link these together into a mental map. Use your ears and nose, too. You may be able to tell where you are by the changing sounds of a distant creek. Learn to use available resources. (May 93, p.56)

The reflection from even a small mirror can be seen for miles. Lost hunters have used mirrors, shiny pieces of metal or aluminum foil to attract the attention of search planes, boats and even workers in distant fire towers. Hold the mirror next to your eye with one hand, and extend your other hand in the direction you want to send the light flashes. By sighting through the hole in the mirror (if it is a signal-type mirror), or just over the top, you can aim the light to hit your extended hand, and sweep it to the target (airplane, boat, etc.). Waggle the light quickly back and forth, to your hand and to the target, to attract attention. (May 93, p.56)

Keep track of time and gauge how fast you are moving. Putting these variables together, you can judge roughly how far you've traveled—and how long it will take to return to your starting point. (May 93, p.56)

Search-and-rescue agencies often equip crews with night vision goggles, so if lost try to get some kind of light going at night. Chemical sticks work well, as do pocket-sized strobes. A flashlight also will do the job. (May 93, p.57)

Stamp out messages in the snow. The most common is SOS, but a huge X is easier to make. Make the signal big—100 feet to each letter isn't too large. In snow, line one edge of the letters with green boughs or burnt sticks to increase the contrast. One stranded boater used white rocks to spell out SOS on a dark beach.

With a steady breeze, you can roughly gauge your direction of travel. Obviously, that's worthless if the wind is swirling, or if it changes drastically. But over the short haul, a steady breeze works pretty well as a poor man's compass.

Make one or more big signal fires. The smoke should contrast with the background. Make black smoke by putting oily rags or pieces of rubber tire on the fire. Make white smoke by adding green leaves, moss or a little water to the fire. Keep the materials for the fire built up, but don't light it until you see or hear potential rescuers. Always carry waterproof matches or a fire starter. (May 93, p.57)

Lay out straight lines of clothes, tents and other gear. Wave a bright shirt on the end of a pole when you hear airplanes. Get out in the open. Make big signals. And remain determined that you will get someone's attention. (May 93, p.57)

Hunters who rely on magnetic compasses should set their gun down while taking a reading. The amount of iron in the average firearm is enough to alter the compass reading.

This shelter is simple. The snow trench can easily be made and will keep you alive in a life-threatening situation. Dig the trench 2½ to 3 feet deep, using a snowshoe, frying pan, forked stick, even your hands if necessary, just long enough and wide enough for your body, adding a deeper cold sink section at the foot end. Line the bottom and sides with evergreen boughs. Cover the top with a weighted tarp or by thatching a frame of natural materials, then roofing it with boughs or snow-slabs. The trench's insulated environment will be considerably warmer than the air above. (July 95, p.75)

Constructing the shear-pole shelter. One end of the ridgepole rests on the ground, the other end is lashed to two vertical poles in a reverse-V configuration. In cold weather, make it just large enough to hold your body, and keep a fire going near the entrance. If you lack cordage, rest the ridgepole in the fork of a tree. (July 95, p.75)

U nless you're being chased by a bear, by bandits or by a landslide, stop immediately if you sprain your ankle. In the backcountry put your foot in a cold stream or pack it in snow. If its available, use ice wrapped in a moistened cloth. If the sprain is bad, much swelling and discoloration, you should rest and elevate the ankle for 48 hours, icing it three or four times a day. (June 92, p.20)

T o survive a lightning storm, the best shelter is in a low area of forest under a thick stand of small trees. Do not seek a clearing, since you become the tallest object in it and are more likely to be struck. (June 92, p.20)

I t is best not to be in the woods during an electrical storm, but if you are unable to avoid this situation, knowing your trees may save your life. Oaks, particularly  the red oak family, attract lightning due to the tanning in the bark. Beech trees, on the other hand are seldom struck by lightning. (May 93, p.76)